A PRACTICAL APPROACH TO LIFE SATISFACTION

A PRACTICAL APPROACH TO LIFE SATISFACTION

Powered by Emotional Knowledge and Grit

ROBERT OTT

Copyright © 2022 Robert Ott.

All rights reserved. No part of this book may be used or reproduced by any means, graphic, electronic, or mechanical, including photocopying, recording, taping or by any information storage retrieval system without the written permission of the author except in the case of brief quotations embodied in critical articles and reviews.

This book is a work of non-fiction. Unless otherwise noted, the author and the publisher make no explicit guarantees as to the accuracy of the information contained in this book and in some cases, names of people and places have been altered to protect their privacy.

Archway Publishing books may be ordered through booksellers or by contacting:

Archway Publishing
1663 Liberty Drive
Bloomington, IN 47403
www.archwaypublishing.com
844-669-3957

Because of the dynamic nature of the Internet, any web addresses or links contained in this book may have changed since publication and may no longer be valid. The views expressed in this work are solely those of the author and do not necessarily reflect the views of the publisher, and the publisher hereby disclaims any responsibility for them.

Any people depicted in stock imagery provided by Getty Images are models, and such images are being used for illustrative purposes only.
Certain stock imagery © Getty Images.

ISBN: 978-1-6657-1674-1 (sc)
ISBN: 978-1-6657-1676-5 (hc)
ISBN: 978-1-6657-1675-8 (e)

Library of Congress Control Number: 2021925652

Print information available on the last page.

Archway Publishing rev. date: 1/31/2022

For my parents' unconditional support
throughout the years.

We must be willing to get rid of the life we've planned,
so as to have the life that is waiting for us.
—Joseph Campbell

CONTENTS

Foreword xi

Part 1: Empirical Evidence for the Intersections among Grit, Emotional Intelligence, and Life Satisfaction

Chapter 1	Introduction 1
Chapter 2	What Causes Life Dissatisfaction? 32
Chapter 3	My Story 52
Chapter 4	A Novel Study on Grit, Emotional Intelligence (EI), and Life Satisfaction 125

Part 2: Cultivating Grit and Emotional Intelligence to Improve Life Satisfaction

Chapter 5	Learning Grit, Expanding Emotional Intelligence 149
Chapter 6	Passion 160
Chapter 7	Perseverance 179
Chapter 8	Consistency 197

Conclusion 209
Bibliography 215

FOREWORD

Robert's work is like a fine blend of a very good wine to be sipped, swirled about, and enjoyed over time. I've known Dr. Robert Ott for almost eight years. He came into the Academic Institute (AIE) at Indian River State College to learn how to use the Learning Management System. I watched Robert quickly grasp new information and put it to use. When he couldn't figure out a required process, he knew where and how to reach for technical assistance and then apply the information to both his face-to-face and online learning environments.

In 2016, I was fortunate to be a part of the flawless trip he planned and executed for thirty-eight fantastic people, twenty-five of whom were exceptional high school students, to Europe! Ms. Alessandra, our tour guide from the moment we landed in Rome, gracefully gave way as she too listened and learned from her storytelling "client." For the next fifteen days, Robert Ott educated and entertained this entire traveling contingency with facts and rumored anecdotes about kings, queens, tyrants, and heroes, recalling names and soliloquies from the ancient Senate floor near the Roman Colosseum to historical ramifications of the decisions from the Vatican and the explicit horrors of the death camps of Germany. His words and enthusiasm brought history to life for everyone who had the privilege to hear his active recreations.

As a high school teacher, I've seen how his students trust his words and acts of both fairness and kindness in the classroom as they seek transparency, acceptance, and relevant information with Dr. Ott as their instructor for multiple courses, such as student success and AP psychology. He has taught over ninety classes at Indian River State College, with subjects ranging from human development and psychology to student success.

His passion for teaching is omnipresent and permeates his writing style, reaching the active reader through active and provocative, personal ways. The reading seamlessly employs his extensive applicable knowledge of literature, world history, and financial literacy, weaving his tale of strengths and accomplishments while exposing his life of perilous lows and delirious highs. His personal journey of discovery is supported with emotional tours as he measures his own contentment of life and accomplishments through the triangulation of grit, growth mindset, and emotional intelligence.

My friend and colleague Dr. Ott is passionate about how to help his readers achieve their individual paths of success. Supported with an extraordinary amount of empirical evidence, he weaves the reader through a cross-cultural exploration of how people throughout the ages have studied the effect of how true success can be measured. For example, in an attempt to define what is found in the Finnish culture, you will explore *sisu*, the elusive latent power of a person. Through historical studies in psychological advancements of Francis Galton and his study of ties between ability, passion, and hard labor, to the most current references of Angela Duckworth and her findings of grit, perseverance, and growth mindset, readers are treated to a thorough exploration and careful explanation of what passionate professionals have discovered and documented. These references are present, footnoted, and available for your own perusal for further study.

Then through a hands-on approach, Robert provides guided activities that will ask readers to activate their own positive potential, exposing the innate tools of personal power as he provides a guided pathway for readers to participate in your own journey and to define and create your path to life satisfaction.

I hope you enjoy this journey of self-discovery and internal reflection of how and why you can find, define, and deserve life satisfaction. Be educated. Get motivated. Find and define your *sisu*, and like a fine wine, sip and enjoy the read.

Sincerely,
Michael Pelitera, EdM
Indian River State College
PS: friend and colleague of Dr. Robert Ott

PART ONE

Empirical Evidence for the Intersections among
Grit, Emotional Intelligence, and Life Satisfaction

CHAPTER 1

Introduction

When we think about the quality of our lives, it probably goes without saying that we all want to be satisfied. This degree of life satisfaction is more than a transient state of happiness. The concept of life satisfaction implies a deep, abiding, and overarching sense of contentment with the lives we lead, which persists despite the challenges we experience. Often, the idea of life satisfaction can feel tied to circumstance. While many of us fall into the trap by saying, "If I only had X, or achieved Y, I would be happy." We should avoid unrealistic comparisons while remembering that we cannot fill a void with intangible items or people to improve our happiness.

Nevertheless, fewer people consciously acknowledge knowing that active tools and behaviors may advance our contentment with life on a practical and lasting level. The purpose of this book is to provide evidence-based research and practical recommendations that will enable you to hone the tools of emotional intelligence with grit to achieve life satisfaction. While we'll unpack each of the concepts, the first point of order to address is that the ultimate goal of this book's advice is not achievement per se but contentment and well-being. Of course, honing skills of perseverance, passion, and consistency will help you achieve your goals. However, the paradigm shift from achievement to life satisfaction is key to this book's aims. By developing *emotionally intelligent* versions of grit components, achievements become a waypoint—even a beneficial by-product—of the journey toward a more holistic form of life satisfaction.

When most people think about the concept of "grit," it is about hard work, productivity, and overcoming obstacles to achieve both short- and long-term goals. Grit is associated with perseverance, passion, and consistency, which—particularly in our achievement-oriented culture—tend to have connotations related to pursuing career, financial, or personal success. While both academic studies and personal development texts have addressed the use of grit in relation to human performance, its role in life satisfaction has received very little attention. However, when grit works together with emotional intelligence, it yields marked improvements in life satisfaction. This thought prompts a fundamental question. Can we create and cultivate the type of grit and emotional intelligence that will help us achieve our goals while improving our satisfaction with life?

Before answering this question, it is essential to define the key concepts at play, a brief overview of research related to the topic, and recommendations for using this book. Notably, this book constitutes a novel intervention in current research with advice on this subject. As a result, this book brings grit and emotional intelligence into the academic conversation to delineate their effect on life satisfaction rather than achievement. Therefore, the following section provides brief definitions of the relevant concepts to explain what each concept means individually before piecing them together into an applicable framework.

Definitions
Grit

Philosophers have long tried to explain human performance. Eventually, the discipline of psychology was born from the related field of ancient philosophy. From as early as the nineteenth century, researchers utilized the scientific method to research factors that could help explain the success of some individuals but not others. Early research pioneers wondered why some people seem to excel and others do not, even when there are no easily discernable differences between them. Many have attempted to explain the individual differences in success to talent. The reason for this is obvious. It is much more palatable to suggest that more successful individuals have achieved their aims because they have an ineffable, innate quality that has enabled them to do so. Human nature means that we—scholars included—would prefer to suggest, "She has more talent and intelligence than I do," than imagine, "She works harder than I do and cares more than I about achieving her aims."

More recently though, researchers have suggested that factors like hard work and dedication tend to play a more significant role than those indefinable and innate qualities like "talent" and IQ. Indeed, fields of psychology and self-help tend to favor theories that focus on behaviors and their concrete causes rather than on innate and difficult-to-discern traits. Most notably, for the purposes of this study, Angela Duckworth proposed the concept of *grit* to explain individuals' ability to persevere toward long-term goals—while retaining interest and passion in a project—even in the presence of obstacles and challenges.[1] While Duckworth's work and how her study relates to this one will be discussed in chapter 3, it is most important to note that grit is not innate. Instead, it is a skill that can be improved and developed throughout your lifetime. It is not a "You have it or you don't" concept.

---

[1] Angela L. Duckworth et al., "Grit: Perseverance and Passion for Long-Term Goals," *Journal of Personality and Social Psychology* 92, no. 6 (2007): 1087–1101.

It requires only passion. Passion is understood as consistent, sustained interest in an endeavor over some time and perseverance. Perseverance is the ability to show up consistently and to work hard.

If you've just read this statement and thought, *But I find myself lacking in passion* or *I struggle with giving up on my goals when things get difficult*, this book is for you. Passion and perseverance are not unattainable or inherent characteristics but traits that can be developed at any time and in any area of life. Notably, the tools of grit are applicable to work or academic domains and apply to the pursuit of hobbies, parenting and relationships, and educational capacities, among other applications. Significantly and uniquely, as a concept, grit tends to allow for an even broader range of applications than other similar psychological characteristics.

The Philosophy of Grit

"In both philosophy and psychology," ethical researchers have argued, "many have found it helpful to liken the will to a muscle, in that it can be stronger or weaker, toughened with exercise over time, and depleted with overuse."[2] So while my expertise and the direction of this book overall are psychology-centric, developing our understanding of grit through a more theoretical, philosophical lens makes sense. Moreover, this concept of grit as a muscle is a helpful metaphor to ground our notion of the concept. Finally, it illustrates one of the fundamental tenets of this book: your grit can be improved in the same way as your abdominal muscles. Not without effort or endurance, but it is not an inherent characteristic that you must do without if you lack now. Quite the reverse, in fact.

However, as Morton and Paul point out, while the idea of will as a muscle alludes to the fact that we have the capacity to develop grit over time, the metaphor lacks something of a complete philosophical understanding of grit, the crux of which is why some people tend to

---

[2] Jennifer M. Morton and Sarah K. Paul, "Grit," *Ethics* 129, no. 2 (2019): 176.

give up in the face of obstacles while others persist and eventually succeed. Excepting circumstances in which individuals reevaluate the value of their intended action was of interest to Morton and Paul. They aimed to discover why some individuals have more of a tendency to abandon their goals than others. As a result, they worked from the hypothesis that "in many cases the failure to persevere has an epistemic explanation: it is attributable to a significant decrease in confidence that one is likely to succeed if one continues to try."[3] While this philosophical thought experiment differentiates the idea of the will as muscle from the more complex concept of grit, the idea of confidence is also key to my overall premise in this book: that grit can be developed with the right knowledge and appropriately applied effort. However, this with the caveat that there is a certain amount of confidence—grounded in the belief that it is possible to grow your grit—required before this becomes true.

Noting the importance of hope and optimism to the achievement of grit (and citing researchers like Martin Seligman and Angela Duckworth), Morton and Paul move into the more philosophical and ethical realm. They suggested, "Take it to be a virtue if the epistemic dimension of grit can be vindicated without appeal to the controversial assumption that we can or should hold our beliefs on the basis of considerations showing them to be useful or good."[4] Interestingly, this type of idea takes grit from the idea of being "good for you," which is what we will focus most on in this book, to being inherently "good." While the more important application of this idea is that grit can help you achieve your aims and advance your life satisfaction. It is also worth highlighting that developing grit can be considered—from a philosophical perspective—more objectively and broadly "good" or even an ethical pursuit.

These ethical scholars suggested that people who lack grit tend to give up on activities based on "sour grapes" or adverse experiences that

---

[3] Morton and Paul, "Grit," 178.
[4] Morton and Paul, "Grit," 179.

don't change the individual's perspective. Rather than changing the value of their goal, they decide to give up entirely. More specifically, they note that such instances "may count as a failure of grit, in that grit involves the avoidance of sour grapes."[5] They note too that grit often requires some degree of irrationality because it is closely associated with perseverance in the face of immense obstacles. In other words, in a philosophical sense, grit has to involve a degree of pushing "sour grapes" and logic itself aside in favor of moving toward a goal. They suggested that "grit must be a matter of persevering even though one assigns a higher expected utility to another option, or of maintaining optimism by ignoring or failing to respond rationally to any countervailing evidence."[6] They do not suggest that grit cannot be rational, but that "just as we have need of the ability to make lasting commitments in the face of equally or incomparably valuable alternatives, we have need of the ability to make lasting commitments that can survive periods in which one's prospects appear gloomy."[7] Thus, grit is a delicate mental balance that involves choices—whether rational or irrational—rather than innate skills or talents. Suppose we begin to conceptualize grit as a series of intelligent decisions concerning our perseverance and sustained levels of passion. In that case, we can ignore sour grapes, overlook the easiest or even most logical option, and persist even when prospects are dim. As a result, we realize that we have all the agency we need to grow grit even when it hasn't been present in us before.

We can think of grit as a way of exhibiting confidence in ourselves and our will to succeed rather than thinking of it as a lack of logic. Rather "as long as an action is up to the agent and he has sincerely resolved to do it, he ought to believe that he will do it—even if there is substantial evidence suggesting otherwise."[8] Philosophically, we might think of grit as this type of radical belief in ourselves. And

---

[5] Morton and Paul, "Grit," 181.
[6] Morton and Paul, "Grit," 182.
[7] Morton and Paul, "Grit," 185.
[8] Morton and Paul, "Grit," 187.

importantly, hope and optimism are crucial to such ideas of confidence and success. The researchers note, "Perhaps the gritty agent need not actually believe that success is likely, or have a reasonably high credence in the proposition that she will succeed; she need merely be licensed to reason and act as though she does."[9] Again, this suggests that finding cause for hope in the ultimate achievement of a goal is key to sustaining grit over time.

The researchers ultimately propose an evidential threshold to explain how grit can operate without contravening logic. Still, for our purposes, the reason for attending to the philosophy of grit is to account for a more abstract view than that usually addressed in the psychology field of how it functions and affects individual behavior. Moreover, by building our understanding of grit on its ethical and philosophical implications, we are more equipped to understand that it involves a delicate balance of logic, self-belief, risk management, and hope. More importantly, if we apply these ideas of the philosophy of grit in our own lives, we can engage in a crucial process of self-reflection that will help us understand how we currently exhibit or fail to exhibit grit and how to improve it.

Grit-Adjacent Concepts

The term *grit* may feel familiar as a casual descriptor—perhaps alongside *rugged* or *tough*—of a person or film but more abstract as a psychological concept with its ineffable qualities. Indeed, it was not until I became a psychologist that I understood how grit, emotional intelligence, and life satisfaction are interrelated. Grit is fast becoming a well-studied, noncognitive construct in the field of positive psychology and adjacent specialties. In addition to philosophy, as discussed in the previous section, and positive psychology in the school of Angela Duckworth—as I'll discuss in more detail throughout this book—there

---

[9] Morton and Paul, "Grit," 197.

are understandings of grit (sometimes by other names) in both other fields and in various cultures.

In *The Finnish Way*, Katja Pantzar addresses the Finnish attitude to activities and lifestyle choices that involve a high degree of resilience and mental fortitude. Most emblematically perhaps, the practice of winter swimming in frigid, nearly Arctic waters is closely related to the concept of sisu. She quotes a friend, Tiina, who explains the ubiquitous Finnish concept as involving "a kind of daily stamina and resilience to keep everything running, even through life's gray patches."[10] Even at this early stage in our process of understanding grit, this definition should feel extremely familiar. However, this offhand description of a well-known cultural concept connects quite closely with the consistency of passion and perseverance grit requires and accounts for the need to sustain this type of attitude in both positive and negative circumstances throughout life.

In further attempting to understand the Finnish concept of sisu, Pantzar cites an article concerning "the glossary of happiness." This article addresses the story of how the term *sisu* inspired positive psychologist Tim Lomas to create and catalog words with favorable traits to sisu with no exact equivalency in English. As a result, the lexicography now contains words that are comparable to sisu. The article noted, "Sisu is similar to what an American might call perseverance or the trendier concept of grit, but it has no real equivalent in English." Furthermore, while it alluded to the fact that the term described a universal human quality, it is recognized particularly well by this untranslatable term in Finnish.[11]

This positive lexicography project was inspired by a talk by Emilia Lahti, a former student of Angela Duckworth. Her academic work focuses on the concept of sisu. Lathti first broadly defines sisu as "an age-old Finnish cultural construct traditionally used to describe the

---

[10] Katja Pantzar, *The Finnish Way* (New York: TarcherParigree, 2018), 23.
[11] Emily Anthes, "The Glossary of Happiness," *The New Yorker*, May 12, 2016, https://www.newyorker.com/tech/annals-of-technology/the-glossary-of-happiness.

ability of individuals to push through unbearable challenges"[12] and notes that it has been used to describe Finnish ethnic heritage and similar concepts. Its derivation is from *sisus*, or the guts of the human or animal body, and—as Lahti notes—has generally been pervasive in Finnish culture and in descriptions of it but was critically lacking in empirical research. Therefore, Lahti attempted to conduct research to understand what sisu is and whether it should be considered a positive quality. Based on a survey of 1,208 people, Lahti identified the themes they used most frequently to define the term, breaking the primary themes into three categories: extraordinary perseverance, action mindset, and latent power.

Lahti describes the first theme, extraordinary perseverance, as the process of "extending oneself during a moment of suffering or significant discomfort,"[13] exceeding preconceived individual capacities, and overcoming significant (rather than everyday) adversities. It comprises behaviors and ideas including not giving up, finishing what one starts, enduring hardship, exceeding oneself, doing the impossible, having integrity, and refusing to take shortcuts. While perhaps still more extreme and colorfully described, this should be viewed as very closely attuned to the concept of perseverance so crucial to the idea of grit.

Action mindset is characterized by a "consistent, courageous approach towards challenges" and by "the tendency to lean into the unknown and even seek out situations that are likely to test the individual."[14] In close relation to the philosophical idea of grit's tenuous relationship to the rational likelihood of success, Lahti also describes this aspect of sisu as "taking action when there is no guarantee of success, and, in fact, failure may seem the likely outcome. It is about the beliefs and mindsets that pave the way toward action in situations that

---

[12] Emilia Lahti, "Embodied Fortitude: An Introduction to the Finnish Construct of Sisu." International Journal of Wellbeing 9, no. 1 (2019): 62.
[13] Lahti, "Embodied Fortitude," 65.
[14] Lahti, "Embodied Fortitude," 66.

may at first seem overpowering and impossible. In this sense, it can even be seen as a catalyst for exceeding our preconceived capacities."[15] Again, and in this instance linked to an embodied Finnish notion of gut and courage, this quote should encourage us to think about the cultivable human characteristic of pushing against immense odds, even when success seems (or even is) out of reach. Lahti notes that this action mindset involves boldness, facing one's fears, standing up, creativity resulting from hardship, believing in oneself, and having guts.

While both extraordinary perseverance and action mindset resonate particularly with grit's perseverance dimension and the idea of maintaining consistency in the face of obstacles, it is also worth addressing the third dimension Lahti identified as a key part of sisu: latent power. The most ambiguous or "magical" of the themes, the idea of latent power is most useful for our purposes in grounding the notion that a mindset and actions that lead to more success and higher levels of life satisfaction can be found cultivated *internally*. Lahti defines the term as "an inner power potential that exists for every human being and can be accessed when we have consumed our preconceived mental or physical capacities. At the heart of the action, that manifests as perseverance, courage, and determination. More visceral and somatic than cognitive and conscious." She describes it as an innate quality, at the moment, magic, a spare tank, listless strength, transformation, and the second wind.[16] I think this aspect of sisu is related to the passion element of grit but goes even further to define the engine that powers perseverant actions as visceral and somatic.

Importantly, the second part of Lahti's argument is designed to evaluate whether sisu is always good to exhibit. She identifies a few potential pitfalls of such a gritty attitude to life: physical or mental danger to the self if limits are not acknowledged, harm to others through lack of sympathy to their difficult circumstances or disconnectedness,

---

[15] Lahti, "Embodied Fortitude," 67.
[16] Lahti, "Embodied Fortitude," 67.

and harm to the individual's reasoning or not knowing when to quit (the Sisyphean trap of rolling the boulder up the hill repeatedly for it to roll back down each time). Similarly, scholars had used the scarcity theory to explain how low satisfaction levels surfaced when individuals could not balance the demands associated with nonwork and work activities. This work-life imbalance contributed to role conflicts for work and nonwork activities that led to cognitive conflict.[17] Finally, on a more practical and anecdotal level, one only has to consider the biographies of ultrasuccessful individuals in their various fields like Albert Einstein or Ernest Hemingway. They achieved a great deal of success but at the expense of their mental health and personal relationships. For instance, by the time Hemingway earned the Nobel Prize for Literature in 1954, he had demonstrated true grit by enduring an injury of war, witnessing the Spanish Civil War, and writing fifteen groundbreaking volumes of literature. Yet by 1961, he had divorced three women and died by suicide. Grit—defined as persistence and passion despite obstacles—has received much attention, yet books on this theme often idolize goals like the Nobel Prize at the expense of mental health.

Again, this understanding of grit and sisu has an interesting resonance with the philosophical question about whether possessing grit necessitates abandoning or pushing aside logic in favor of the hope of success. These potential issues, which can apply to grit and sisu, are another argument in favor of my perspective on life satisfaction as the primary outcome measure rather than success. While an overabundance of sisu or grit can produce extremely adverse outcomes if applied too steadfastly to pursue a goal or aim, it is not marked by the same pitfalls if its end goal is life satisfaction. Suppose our aim

---

[17] Stephen R. Marks, "Multiple Roles and Role Strain: Some Notes on Human Energy, Time and Commitment," *American Sociological Review* 42, no. 6 (1977): 921–936, doi:10.2307/2094577; Stephen R. Marks and Shelley M. MacDermid, "Multiple Roles and the Self: A Theory of Role Balance," *Journal of Marriage and Family* 58, no. 2 (1996): 417–432. doi:10.2307/353506.

is enhancing our satisfaction with life with achievements as ideal by-products rather than a single-minded focus on achievement at the expense of everything else. In that case, such outcomes are much less likely to occur.

Ultimately, sisu is not exactly the same as grit but is undoubtedly worth addressing as an adjacent term.

> Sisu overlaps with certain endurance aspects of perseverance and grit but differs in its emphasis on short-term intensity rather than long-term stamina. Most of the examples of sisu in the data involved determination and doggedness typical of grit but without the passion or focus for a big, overarching life goal. Sisu is less about passion, achievement and winning (although it definitely can relate to those situations as well) and more about "putting up a good fight" and giving something everything you have. Grit and perseverance get us on the road and keep us going long. Sisu is the spare tank of fuel we tap into when we find ourselves running on empty.[18]

Interestingly, this idea of sisu not being about achievement or winning should indicate that, by pairing grit with life satisfaction rather than achievement, we can take the term slightly further into the gut-bound, magical elements of sisu. So whether your goal is to take up winter swimming or not, it is worth pausing over the similarities of the concepts of sisu and grit, partly because of the similarities between sisu and the grit factor. And why the grit factor is an important concept on which this book is largely based. The underlying ideas are still broader, as are the human characteristics that can develop across time and space.

---

[18] Lahti, "Embodied Fortitude," 72.

Broad Applications of Grit

While grit is far from the only aim of this book, I'd like to pause here as well to illustrate what I mean about grit having applications for domains outside the typical outcomes of achievement in work or school. Binding to the paradigm shift I'm advocating from achievement to life satisfaction is grit's capacity to apply to other domains of life. At the same time, I will provide much more detail on different dimensions of grit and their application throughout the rest of this book. My purposes in this definitional section are to emphasize the broad-ranging nature of grit and its applications. Grit is not innate, fixed, or unattainable. Rather, it can be nurtured, strengthened, and developed over time and with effort.

One example of both is the application of the grit mindset to interpersonal relationships. Also based in part on interactions with Angela Duckworth, Jon and Kathryn Gordon published a book applying the idea of grit particularly to its role in sustaining intimate relationships. The preface notes that "if *two people* are committed to making it work and have relationship grit, you'll not only stay together, you'll learn so much more about yourselves, discover a lot of life lessons along the way, grow as individuals, and become stronger as a team."[19] The book progresses through how to apply different concepts of grit to various relationship challenges. It indicates that scholars and self-help writers alike are emphasizing the varied applicability of grit to different domains.

Similarly, Berislav Marušić has addressed commitment and, like the ethical article on grit, examined the interplay between belief in one's success and rationality.[20] Most notably for our purposes, Marušić cites three paradigmatic examples of commitment. These commitments aren't related to work or traditionally conceived

---

[19] Jon Gordon and Kathryn Gordon, *Relationship Grit: A True Story with Lessons to Stay Together, Grow Together, and Thrive Together* (Newark: John Wiley & Sons, 2020),

[20] Berislav Marušić, *Evidence and Agency: Norms of Belief for Promising and Resolving* (Oxford: Oxford University Press, 2015).

achievement: maintaining a loyal marriage, quitting smoking, and running a marathon. In addition to vocational and relational goals then, this should indicate that grit—as we'll come to understand and develop throughout the rest of this book—can likewise be a useful tool for anything that requires commitment, including health and exercise-based aims, parenting challenges, the pursuit of hobbies and passion projects, and countless other areas of life.

Emotional Intelligence

To truly power the tools of grit, it is first necessary to define and develop emotional intelligence. As mentioned in the previous section, the development of the intelligence quotient (IQ) idea dovetailed with scholars' interest in what separates the highly successful few from the suboptimally performing many. Psychologists have long noted the importance of intelligence. Still, more recently, researchers have accorded increasing attention to *intelligence domains*—not just the stereotypical idea of overall mental intelligence but also versions like kinesthetic, spatial, and musical bits of intelligence. Emotional intelligence includes knowledge and skills people acquire due to their interpersonal and intrapersonal interactions with others.

First used as a term in 1964, emotional intelligence emerged as a new idea related to accepted concepts like social skills and empathy.[21] Interestingly, "researchers in the field quickly settled into two camps. One conceptualised emotional intelligence as a trait, in line with personality theory; that is, as a behavioural disposition best measured via self-report … The other school focused on considering EI as a set of related skills, akin to cognitive ability, measured through performance on specific tasks."[22] In this book, I take the second view, which has

---

[21] Michael Beldoch, "Sensitivity to Expression of Emotional Meaning in Three Modes of Communication," *The Communication of Emotional Meaning*, ed. J. R. Davitz and Michael Beldoch (Columbus, OH: McGraw-Hill; 1964), 31–42.

[22] Paul A. Tiffin and Lewis W. Paton, "When I Say … Emotional Intelligence," *Medical Education* 54, no. 7 (2020): 598–599, 598.

come to be widely accepted by many scholars of emotional intelligence, that the concept can be learned and developed as a skill.

More specifically, emotional intelligence refers to an individual's ability to perceive emotions accurately and the feelings of other individuals in proximity while self-regulating emotions based on environmental demands and contextual pressures. Emotional intelligence is used in psychological research to describe the emotional knowledge acquired through relationships among groups of people. Emotional intelligence is a cognitive trait that researchers measure across five dimensions.[23] These elements help us build empathy, which improves our social skills and motivation partly because we become more self-aware before regulating behavior. The first dimension measures people's capacity to comprehend their own emotions. The second dimension measures people's ability to accurately evaluate the feelings of others with whom they interact. The third dimension measures people's ability to regulate their emotions by seeking out situations that make them happier, enabling them to exercise an amount of control over their feelings. The fourth dimension measures people's ability to regulate the emotions of others by arranging activities that make them happier and more confident. Finally, the fifth dimension measures people's ability to use positive emotions to develop new ideas during moments when obstacles make it more challenging to remain productive.

Susan David, a Harvard Medical School psychologist and author of the 2016 book *Emotional Agility*, focuses in her TED talk on the importance of avoiding a cult of positivity and instead we should accept all of our emotions.

> Research now shows that the radical acceptance of all of our emotions—even the messy, difficult ones— is the cornerstone to resilience, thriving, and true,

---

[23] Kevin A. Davies et al., "Validity and Reliability of a Brief Emotional Intelligence Scale (BEIS-10)," *Journal of Individual Differences* 31, no. 4 (2010): 198–208.

authentic happiness. But emotional agility is more than just an acceptance of emotions. We also know that accuracy matters. In my own research, I found that words are essential. We often use quick and easy labels to describe our feelings. "I'm stressed" is the most common one I hear. But there's a world of difference between stress and disappointment or stress and that knowing dread of "I'm in the wrong career." When we label our emotions accurately, we are more able to discern the precise cause of our feelings. And what scientists call the readiness potential in our brain is activated, allowing us to take concrete steps. But not just any steps—the right steps for us. Because our emotions are data.[24]

David's idea of emotional intelligence as agility and emotions as data highlights the idea that emotional intelligence can work as a functional and adaptable tool with multiple dimensions of efficacy.

I'll discuss the dimensions of emotional intelligence in more detail in the sections to which they pertain. Even now, the most important aspect of this definition for our purposes is that emotional intelligence applies to oneself and others. Not only does it entail your ability to discern how you are feeling and why, but it also enables you to gain insight into the emotions of others. It facilitates self-regulation of your own emotions and constitutes the tools with which you can effect change regarding the emotions of others. In other words, this means that the tools of emotional intelligence—and by extension those of emotionally intelligent grit—can be used not only in personal development, vocational goals, and other individual pursuits but also in cultivating relationships, educating others, and parenting.

---

[24] Susan David, "The Gift and Power of Emotional Courage," filmed November 2017 in New Orleans, LA. TED video, 16:30, https://www.ted.com/talks/susan_david_the_gift_and_power_of_emotional_courage.

Applications of Emotional Intelligence

As a broad and holistic concept, the idea of emotional intelligence can appear somewhat vague and abstract at first glance. You may think of it only on an interpersonal level and of being described as "emotionally intelligent," akin to being described as "compassionate," "kind," "sympathetic," or "emotionally mature." While these aspects may indeed be part of the concept, I'd like to emphasize that emotional intelligence—like grit—is not a personality trait that one either possesses or lacks. Instead, it is a set of functional tools that can change our behaviors and interactions with others in various arenas and power our pursuit of life satisfaction. Usually the term is thrown around in mysterious ways in society and popular culture. For instance, an annoyed ex-partner may regale their friends with stories that illustrate that the relationship fell apart because the other party was "lacking in emotional intelligence." Perhaps an acquaintance acted in an obtuse and disrespectful manner toward you, so you casually blamed their unbecoming behavior on a lack of emotional intelligence. There are many ways that people use anecdotal stories to demonstrate that some people have less emotional intelligence than others. My purpose in this section is to provide an overview of some of the applications of emotional intelligence. Rather than being viewed as a broad and ambiguous trait, it can be considered a multifunctional and useful tool.

Perhaps one of the most prevalent applications of emotional intelligence is in the business and entrepreneurial context. In a 2020 book, *Emotional Intelligence for Sales Leadership: The Secret to Building High-Performance Sales Teams*, Colleen Stanley addresses the fact that while sales-focused businesses are constantly focused on finding ways to improve their efficacy in an increasingly competitive market, many firms are overlooking the potential tools of emotional intelligence and its role in sales. Many people in leadership mistakenly acknowledge that emotional intelligence is a "soft skill" without real applicability in the hard-line sales context. Stanley goes on to describe a typical sales situation that is usually addressed through content knowledge. However, she suggested that it may be better achieved through a return to focusing on the so-called soft skill of emotional intelligence.

> When a salesperson misses sales quota, a sales manager's first response is to teach more hard-selling skills, consultative selling skills. These skills are important, and we teach a lot of them. But is the salesperson not asking enough questions during a sales call because he doesn't know the questions to ask? Or is it because he needs to learn better impulse control and self-awareness to understand when and how he gets triggered during a meeting resulting in a product dump?[25]

Presented thus, it makes perfect sense that businesses would be likely to overlook such skills in favor of the bottom line, but also why they mustn't do. Concisely, Stanley presents this as an equation: "Low self-awareness = low other awareness = no connection = no sale."[26] While making sales in this type of context is not everyone's goal, it does help illustrate the implications of emotional intelligence that fall outside the scope of "soft" interactions with other individuals and the obvious relational implications of the term. As well as being important in a romantic relationship or another interpersonal capacity, emotional intelligence is a key competency in the workforce and in specific aspects of job performance, like a sales role.

Similarly, the function of emotional intelligence in business is often addressed with its leadership role. It is most often connected with transformational leadership; transformational leaders are "those who stimulate and inspire followers to both achieve extraordinary

---

[25] Colleen Stanley, *Emotional Intelligence for Sales Leadership: The Secret to Building High-Performance Sales Teams* (New York: HarperCollins Leadership, 2020), para. 15.
[26] Stanley, *Emotional Intelligence for Sales*, para. 20.

outcomes and, in the process, develop their own leadership capacity. Transformational leaders help followers grow and develop into leaders by responding to individual followers' needs by empowering them and by aligning the objectives and goals of the individual followers, the leader, the group, and the larger organization."[27]

Scholars have attempted to glean insight into how they can acknowledge their emotions effectively while responding to their own and others' feelings. This emotional awareness helps them to relate to subordinates and other leaders within the organizational structure. A recent cross-sectional study with 267 participants found that specific aspects of emotional intelligence are key to the efficacy of transformational leadership.[28] For example, a positive tone led to positive emotions when leaders used one-on-one and group coaching. Positive emotions also led to meaningful mentoring with the staff, especially when conflict resolution needed to address problems within departments to avoid production disruptions. Thus, empathy and positive emotions are key characteristics of transformational leaders. In addition, this study has practical implications for entrepreneurs and businesses. They suggested a new criterion that screens recruits during the hiring process for emotional knowledge to create new and effective organizational leaders.

Although emotional intelligence research has long been connected with these types of leadership behaviors, we need experiential leadership within our organizational structures. Experiential leadership is a skill set that hiring managers should screen for before assigning talent to key management roles. The socially changing landscape is changing the organizational structure of companies. This structural agitation disrupts old models, and we need a fresh approach to leadership if companies want to survive. Managing from a data set on a spreadsheet is insufficient given

---

[27] Bernard M. Bass, and Ronald E. Riggio, *Transformational Leadership*, 2nd ed. (Mahwah, NJ: L. Erlbaum Associates, 2006), p. 3.
[28] Gina Gorgens-Ekermans and Chene Roux, "Revisiting the Emotional Intelligence and Transformational Leadership Debate: Does Emotional Intelligence Matter to Effective Leadership?" *SA Journal of Human Resource Management* 19, no. 2 (2021): 1–13, 9.

the complexities of technology and human capital. Instead, executive leaders must move from their comfortable C-suite into an experiential role that moves from theory to applying various skills to existing positions. This logic applies to D-level executives and mid-level managers who manage from afar. As a result, they become disengaged from workers. Shifting to experiential leadership increases overall production while improving department morale when workers feel leadership identifies with them. This feeling of appreciation is exacerbated when workers feel like stakeholders. Afterward, they can create new posts to improve operational outcomes before increasing sales production.

Emotional intelligence has also been studied extensively concerning the field of medicine. Perhaps unsurprisingly, given the importance of bedside manner and interactions with patients, it is crucial for health care professionals to cultivate and practice emotional intelligence. Therefore, many stakeholders in the field have argued that it should be enshrined in curricula as a teachable skill that would-be doctors must learn during medical school.

Further, several studies found that doctors' and patients' medical outcomes improved if they were emotionally intelligent. Encouraging positive emotions and emotional knowledge improved their ability to cope with illness and treatment. Emotional intelligence has been shown to improve clinical competence and communication among health care professionals and help them cope with the challenges of the job. A recent article on emotional intelligence among home health care workers reported, "It is important that clinicians first be able to understand themselves. Emotions can synchronize between nurses and patients, leading to a domino effect, where one person's mood (positive/negative) has a similar effect on others. Thus, our interactions with patients have the potential to lift morale or damage confidence. Recognizing emotions and effectively managing feelings (without denial) require a calm poise in often-volatile situations."[29]

---

[29] Nadine Wodwaski and Renee Courtney, "Emotional Intelligence: An Unspoken Competency in Home Care," *Home Healthcare Now* 38, no. 5 (2020): 286.

While addressed in a particular medical context here, this description is indicative of the importance of emotional intelligence more broadly. It highlights a vital component of the concept: that it relates to both self and others.

Rather than being only applicable to one's interpersonal dealings with other individuals, it is also essential to be aware of one's own emotions. These are both in their own right on the individual and their effect on others. The ability to manage one's own emotions—to self-regulate—is key to my argument in this book. My recommendations teach people how to develop and use the tools of emotional intelligence.

Similar to the field of medicine, numerous studies have addressed the relevance of emotional intelligence to the teaching profession. And in the same way, this learnable skill can relate to home health care settings. There are several benefits to using emotional intelligence as an essential tool. First, it helps practitioners achieve effective teaching while mitigating industry burnout. Second, the practitioners keep their jobs longer. Third, lower turnover meant that the staff experienced higher levels of job satisfaction. Fourth, a more satisfied employee improves job performance and patient care and helps teachers regulate their emotions. As a result of improved emotional outcomes, emotional intelligence is being considered with curricula. Many teachers and parents are engaged in developing strategies for teaching emotional intelligence to others during early childhood and after. A recent article on this topic suggested practical approaches for teachers to use with students when cultivating emotional intelligence. Finally, there are positive benefits to teaching students emotional knowledge. Emotionally knowledgeable students "are better able to pay attention, are more engaged in school, have more positive relationships, and are more empathic."[30]

---

[30] Shauna L. Tominey, Elisabeth C. O'Bryon, Susan E. Rivers, and Sharon Shapses, "Teaching Emotional Intelligence in Early Childhood," *YC Young Children* 72, no. 1 (2017): 6–14, 6.

The practical recommendations section of this book will address this issue in more detail. However, it is essential to note that my focus here is on cultivating emotional intelligence in oneself. This approach accounts for the importance of helping others develop those tools well. Developing one's own emotional intelligence is possible—as a parent, teacher, or caretaker—to help others cultivate those skills as well. In addition to this direct teaching or modeling, the ability to better regulate your own emotions will pay dividends in your interactions with others across the board. While this is only a brief overview of some of the application areas of emotional intelligence, it intends to illustrate how it goes far beyond the stereotypical understanding of the concept. Emotional intelligence relates only to our social and relational interactions with others or a vague idea of compassion or emotional maturity.

The Role of Emotional Intelligence in a Changing World

In addition to more traditional applications of emotional intelligence, like entrepreneurship, medicine, and teaching, the concept has also gained recent attention for its potential role in the changing cultural landscape. Several scholars have addressed its potential future importance. Purushothaman based a portion of his work on an assessment that recorded the changes to social and family life during the last century as part of the aftermath of the industrial revolution. He suggested the criticality of emotional intelligence to helping individuals navigate the technological and digital revolution. Society needs to learn "the ability to manage emotions in a complex, fast-changing and uncertain world is likely to be a significant challenge for the next generation. No effort is too small in building EI competencies in people to navigate through the next industrial revolution."[31] More specifically, the book argues that emotional intelligence will become

---

[31] Rajagopalan Purushothaman, *Emotional Intelligence* (New Delhi: SAGE Publications, 2021), xvi.

even more necessary and even less common as we move further into technological advancement. "A significant part of human interactions is likely to be with machines, thanks to the phenomenal technological innovation in areas such as artificial intelligence, machine learning, robotics, 3D printing, and nanotechnology. Humans are likely to lose touch with how to effectively interact with each other. We have already begun to see symptoms of personal disconnection in our families and in our workplaces."[32] Again, this helps illustrate the broad applicability of emotional intelligence. And the fact that it is a developable and adaptable tool that can play a key role in numerous contexts of work, life, and play.

Similarly, the current global work context—both related to the COVID-19 pandemic and increasing globalization—is causing increasing distance between those who need to collaborate across space and time zones. These changes in the workplace and the way humans collaborate socially are necessitating a new type of emotional intelligence that can translate not only in person but also across platforms like Zoom. A recent article focused on the process of returning to in-person workplaces cited emotional intelligence as the key means by which employers and employees alike should attempt to process and succeed throughout this transition process in several key ways: moving away from a one-size-fits-all attitude to work modalities and reactions to difficult circumstances; increasing awareness of coworkers and subordinates; avoiding judgment; leading with "openness, vulnerability, and active listening"; and developing a support network available to members of management teams.[33] In various ways, emotional intelligence should be considered a tool with broad applicability that can power the change needed in a changing world.

---

[32] Purushothaman, *Emotional Intelligence*, 3.
[33] Harvey Deutschendorf, "5 Ways Emotional Intelligence Can Boost Post-COVID-19 Workplace Communication," *FastCompany*, May 20, 2021, https://www.fastcompany.com/90638435/5-ways-emotional-intelligence-can-boost-post-covid-workplace-communication.

Notably, much of the work addressing emotional intelligence is focused on its role in achievement. This point is definitely true about the connection between emotional intelligence and achievement. However, scholars have a growing consensus that emotional intelligence is more than just a "soft skill." Recently, this cognitive construct is only now being accorded room at the scholarly table. Emotional intelligence includes concepts like IQ, specific competencies, specialized knowledge, and other more tangible and well-known "hard" skills. In their 2011 book, *The EQ Edge: Emotional Intelligence and Your Success*, Stein and Book provide the example of the difference between those who succeed academically in high school—the valedictorian, for instance—and those whose record earlier in life is far from stellar but who go on to have enormously successful careers, attributing this to a failure in the school system to measure individuals' capacity for success adequately and ultimately to the presence of emotional intelligence. While their book focused on success, they do define the term more holistically than some. In addition, they acknowledge the preference for cognitive and analytical intelligence in our contemporary culture.

> Driven by the hot pursuit of science and technology, 20th-century culture long emphasized cognitive intelligence as the cornerstone for progress—just as financial reward has long been considered the primary result of that intelligence. The trouble is that sometimes this equation hasn't worked out as planned, as seen in the question: if you're so smart, why aren't you rich? Only in recent years have we begun to appreciate the powerful links between emotional intelligence and a greater, more satisfying, and more well-rounded definition of success which embraces the workplace, marriage and personal

relationships, social popularity, and spiritual and physical well-being.[34]

I agree entirely with Stein and Book regarding the premise of a more holistic and well-rounded application of emotional intelligence to various aspects of life. My mission in this book is similar since it includes material on the application of grit and emotional intelligence tools to fields outside business or academic success, including those of relationship maintenance, parenting, and the pursuit of other hobbies and passion projects outside one's vocation.

However, and as the next definition section will illustrate, it is possible to take this change in perspective a step further. What I'm advocating is a complete paradigm shift away from making the goal of "achievement" or "success" to that of life satisfaction. Instead, suppose we adopt life satisfaction as our primary aim. In that case, the tools of grit and emotional intelligence will be even more functional and help us even more effectively to achieve our purposes.

Life Satisfaction

This book aligns with an overall shift in the psychology field from consideration of achievement as a primary outcome measure to more attention to the idea of life satisfaction as a primary outcome measure. But again, this certainly does not mean that the cultivation of the skills included in this book will not yield achievements. In fact, the opposite is true. Instead, it means that achievement should not be seen as the primary end goal. More accurately, working toward life satisfaction will yield the same achievement-based outcomes but via a much more satisfying journey.

According to psychological researchers, life satisfaction refers to an individual's overall well-being and happiness, which are cognitively

---

[34] Steven Stein and Howard E. Book, *The EQ Edge: Emotional Intelligence and Your Success* (Mississauga, Onariot: Jossey-Bass, 2011), para. 6.

subjective values determined by their level of satisfaction with their lives.[35] Life satisfaction comprises both work and nonwork domains and is dependent not on externally oriented factors—as achievement can be—but on an individual and subjective perspective. In this sense, a "definition" of life satisfaction is somewhat unnecessary because its definition varies depending on the individual to whose life it pertains. While this section is purposefully concise, I will delve much more deeply into the concept of life satisfaction—in the negative sense—via chapter 2's focus on what causes dissatisfaction with life.

Defining Emotionally Intelligent Grit

Together, the three concepts addressed in the previous section have not been studied before. While several researchers have assessed the importance of grit on achievement, its role in life satisfaction has not yet been adequately addressed. Further, while some scholars have suggested that grit and emotional intelligence could be considered in conjunction, very little work in that vein has been undertaken. Even when grit and emotional intelligence have been addressed together, the primary outcome measure of such investigations has tended to be achievement rather than life satisfaction. To focus on this gap in knowledge, I conducted a novel study (which will be detailed in chapter 4) on grit, emotional intelligence, age, and gender to measure their effect on life satisfaction. Based on the results of my study, I have fine-tuned and developed several concepts associated with the development of emotionally intelligent grit: emotionally intelligent passion, emotionally intelligent perseverance, and emotionally intelligent consistency.

I define emotionally intelligent passion as "self-aware, strong, and sustainable dedication, which can be channeled through self-regulation,

---

[35] Javier C. Vela et al., "Positive Psychology and Mexican American College Students' Subjective Well-being and Depression." *Hispanic Journal of Behavioral Sciences* 38, no. 3 (2016): 324–340.

motivation, and practice and which can be cultivated in others through empathy." This definition will become clearer upon reading the subsequent chapters. Still, it is important to note, overall, that this version of passion is not the tempestuous type often associated with romance but a sustained, stable, and self-regulated interest. In addition, this type of passion is a high level of interest that facilitates continual effort over a long period of time.

I define emotionally intelligent perseverance as the following: "the ability to use emotional stability and self-regulation to identify, come to terms with, and redirect from obstacles to the achievement of short- and long-term goals in all domains of life, which produces a form of perseverance that is both sustainable and satisfying in its own right."

Whereas passion is the overall interest and investment component, perseverance has more to do with how it is possible to redirect after facing a challenge or obstacle. If passion is the track, perseverance is the act of getting back on it after a setback of any kind.

Finally, I define emotionally intelligent consistency as "the engine that powers emotionally intelligent passion and emotionally intelligent perseverance—the day-to-day act of 'showing up' that leads to repeated acts of emotionally intelligent passion and perseverance." While passion and perseverance are more typically framed as the dual components of grit, consistency is important in its implications for the continual practice of emotionally intelligent grit. Emotional intelligence is key to the idea of consistency as it requires frequent actions of emotional self-regulation to function effectively.

Part 1 of this book provides the definitional and research-based reasons why it is useful to develop emotionally intelligent grit in terms of empirical outcomes and research. The remainder of this introduction includes information about how to use this book and who it's for. Then in chapter 3, I discuss my story from adolescence to adulthood through a psychological lens. Later, in chapter 4, I provide a condensed version of the quantitative study that I conducted. This novel study added to and altered the course of the existing literature on the subject of grit, emotional intelligence, and life satisfaction.

Part 2 of this book moves from empirical evidence to its practical application. Extrapolating from the results of my novel study on the concept and other existing research, I delve more deeply into the component parts of emotionally intelligent grit and, more importantly, offer recommendations for how they can be applied in different domains of life. First, chapter 5 provides a transition from the empirical evidence-based material to practical application by clarifying that the concepts addressed here are not innate abilities but competencies that you can cultivate. Second, chapter 6 addresses the concept of emotionally intelligent passion. I clarify the difference between a stereotypical understanding of torrid passion typically associated with romance and instead describe passion as a sustained and sustainable form of dedication.

In chapter 7, I address the concept of emotionally intelligent perseverance. I suggest cultivating this skill can make overcoming obstacles more efficient, less painful and protracted, and perhaps even more pleasurable. Finally, in chapter 8, I describe how consistency can ensure sustainability over time after developing these new skills of emotionally intelligent passion and emotionally intelligent perseverance. Chapters 5, 6, 7, and 8 all follow a similar pattern: an introduction to the concept and existing research around the issue, other concepts that are closely related to the topic at hand, definitions and measures of the competency, its future outcomes, and, finally, practical advice for how it might be applied in different domains of life.

How to Use This Book

Although this book is designed to create a progressive understanding of the concepts at play, it does not follow that there is only one way to use it. Whether your primary interest is in this book's theoretical and empirical components or perhaps you'd prefer to have a firmer knowledge base before moving into practical applications, then reading it from beginning to end will be the most effective process for you. Or if you'd prefer to dive promptly into the practical applications section of the text, you can proceed directly to chapters 5, 6, 7, or 8. Then you can refer to the empirical evidence in chapter 4 using the subheadings as needed and reading the remaining chapters in any order.

However you decide to progress through your reading process, I'd suggest making sure to personally action the practical implications in stages. First, take steps toward growing your emotionally intelligent perseverance. Once you feel that you've begun to make positive changes, you can add actions for cultivating your emotionally intelligent passion, or vice versa. After you feel that these goals are established, move toward maintaining them by using emotionally intelligent consistency. As you do so, remember that this process is a lifelong pursuit that you can use for the rest of your life. You can also use it in all areas of your life rather than a quick fix. Set short-term goals that will help ensure you see the benefits of this work as you go, but remember that the long-term goal is paramount. Further, I'd suggest choosing one domain of life for your first attempt to use your emotionally intelligent grit before progressively expanding to other aspects of your life and goals. The tools in this book are meant to provide long-term, effective progression toward life satisfaction, so taking time to develop them in a sustainable manner will be the most beneficial approach.

Who Can Use This Book

As I've mentioned previously in this chapter, emotional intelligence involves regulating both your own and others' emotions. Thus, it has applications both for self-improvement in emotionally intelligent grit and instilling those competencies in others. In this way, the findings of this book apply to parents, other caregivers, and educators at all levels. Applications of the text for such users can be twofold. First, you can work on the concepts in yourself and cultivate them in others.

So for example, a teacher might find a vocational or other life domain application of emotionally intelligent grit in herself. Second, as a result, teachers can then develop lesson plans based on the recommendations from this book, and their own experience, for their students.

The recommendations in this book apply to any domain in which you have a long-term goal. That can be related to work, self-improvement, hobbies, or relationships. The development of emotionally intelligent grit, for example, can be extremely functional for the long-term goals necessary for an active marriage. Since this is a very broad range of applications, the practical advice sections aim to provide general suggestions based on the concepts explained in each chapter and several specific examples. I've attempted to ensure that these examples span various domains. Still, overall, the concepts can be applied to marital, vocational, personal, educational, and parenting arenas as well as any other domain of life you wish. Work on emotional intelligence is uniquely suited to various and widespread applications, given that it is based heavily on self-reflection, empathy, and the regulation of emotions.

Potential Outcomes

Before concluding this chapter, it is worth noting several potential outcomes you may experience as you work toward cultivating emotionally intelligent grit. While these will be addressed in much more detail in chapters 6, 7, and 8, it is worth providing a preview of some of the outcomes you can expect after learning and applying the concepts in this book. Developing emotionally intelligent passion may enable you to move from ephemeral interest in a subject toward a longstanding and a deep sense of purpose for it. Further, passion tends to function as a driving force that enables hard effort; when it is paired with emotional intelligence, you will be able to harness this capacity to your advantage. Finally, contrary to the typical understanding of what passion entails, it enables interest and purpose to be sustained long after the "spark" of your interest in a subject or pursuit has temporarily gone out.

In terms of perseverance, the primary outcome of pairing emotional intelligence with this type of capacity for overcoming obstacles is that rather than feeling out of control when presented with a challenge, you will begin to cope with such challenges more quickly, more efficiently, and even with more enjoyment in the process. While the idea of overcoming challenges with enjoyment may seem alien at this point, the further you delve into your progress through the tools of emotional self-regulation, the more plausible this outcome will seem to become. While life's catastrophes will still feel disastrous, their consequences in terms of taking and keeping you "off track" will be lessened. The primary outcome of fine-tuning your emotionally intelligent consistency is that growing this skill will enable you to maintain the positive changes you implement from this book. This approach will help you continue to use this book to achieve your goals and improve your life satisfaction long after you've turned its last page.

CHAPTER 2

What Causes Life Dissatisfaction?

Before moving to some of the reasons for feeling dissatisfied with life, I conducted a literature review on several key constructs that framed this chapter: grit, emotional intelligence, and life satisfaction. First, it is important to address what causes life dissatisfaction in the first place. At first glance, this point may seem patently obvious. *I'm unhappy because I hate my job* or *I'm unhappy because my marriage is on the rocks* might be among the first typical and broad examples that spring to some people's minds. However, dissatisfaction with life is a much more complicated and nuanced topic than this. In fact, in spite of experiencing immense obstacles and difficulties in their lives, some individuals report their satisfaction with life to be extremely high.

On the other hand, those with ostensibly picture-perfect upbringings and the most advantageous circumstances can be extremely unhappy with their lot. What then makes the difference between those who report very high levels of satisfaction and those who report very low levels? Suppose it is not, or not entirely, based on the most obvious or dramatic points. In that case, we must look elsewhere to unearth the complexity of the subject.

The purpose of this chapter is to provide both a personal and academic discussion of what causes life dissatisfaction. This introduction focuses on examples for different life domains that can contribute to either satisfaction or dissatisfaction in individuals' lives (based on findings from a recent scholarly article on the subject). I will also provide a brief overview of why it's essential to transition from a view of achievement-centric understandings to those related to satisfaction instead. The first section proper of this chapter addresses theories of life satisfaction and life dissatisfaction. It provides a historical overview of research related to life satisfaction, beginning with Freud, whose *Civilization and Its Discontents* is a landmark text in this area. Similarly, Frankl's *Man's Search for Meaning* provides readers a key, broad overview of the subject. Rather than becoming bogged down in dense theoretical material, the purpose of this historical section is to clearly illustrate how previous thinkers have presented their central thoughts on life dissatisfaction in order to help increase your awareness of its stakes in your own life.

After addressing the older psychological material related to individual dissatisfaction, the chapter will transition to the earliest research that used life satisfaction as a term. This work includes the set-point theory by Lykken and Tellegen and the foundational work by Pavot and Diener. Finally, the section progresses to more recent work on life satisfaction, including the reconceptualization of the idea by Headey and Muffels. From different perspectives, all the scholarly work included in this chapter is vital to our purposes in this book. It provides unique insight into why you might need grit and emotional intelligence tools.

To this point, the second section of this chapter will focus on the effects of life dissatisfaction (and its inverse: a high level of life satisfaction). Similarly, and more severely, it will address the connections between depression outcomes and life dissatisfaction. As noted in the introduction to this book, the most effective way to read this theoretical material will be through a process of self-reflection. As you progress through the first two sections of this chapter, be sure to note which parts most resonate with you and use the tools and metrics included to assess your own level of life satisfaction. The more you realize about your starting point and how it connects with the diverse manifestations and ways of thinking about life satisfaction, the more influential the material in part 2 of this book. Again though, the purpose of this material is not to make you feel disheartened about your current levels of life satisfaction. Instead, it's meant to give you new insights into the specific domains in life and ways you're currently experiencing either satisfaction or dissatisfaction with areas of your life. Most importantly, it is essential to emphasize that (as the authors of several of the studies to follow will also do) life satisfaction is not a fixed metric. Instead, its levels tend to fluctuate throughout life as different events occur.

Before moving to the historical and psychological material on life dissatisfaction with a discussion of Freud and Frankl, it is worth noting some of the life domains in which satisfaction or dissatisfaction can occur. We will highlight some of the reasons that life satisfaction functions as a better outcome measure than broadly conceived "success." First, it is essential to note that life satisfaction or dissatisfaction is not a blanket concept. Instead, you may experience high levels of satisfaction in one arena of life but shallow levels of satisfaction in another. Hong surveyed men and women in South Korea.[36] He measured their levels of depression at different stages of life to their reported life satisfaction in other areas: health, family income, residential environment, family relationship, occupation, social relationship, and leisure activities. The results showed the correlation between specific areas of life dissatisfaction

---

[36] Jihyung Hong, "The Areas of Life Dissatisfaction and Their Relationships to Depression at Different Life Stages: Findings from a Nationally Representative Survey," *Psychology, Health & Medicine* 24, no. 3 (2019): 305–319.

and satisfaction (domain-specific measures of life satisfaction) and how they related to overall depression. The results indicate that only health-related dissatisfaction was associated with probable depression across all age groups regardless of gender. Excepting among older men, dissatisfaction with leisure activities also tended to be associated with probable depression.

Significantly about the shift from achievement to satisfaction as a metric, Hong found that dissatisfaction with economic circumstances (income and job) did not actually correlate to probable depression. Relationship satisfaction was paramount among middle-aged and older people. Men relied more on social relationships, and women depended more on familial ones. There are many reasons specific to the academic field of psychology as to why life satisfaction is a better outcome measure than other definitions of success. The reasons it makes sense to make this shift in your own thinking are reasonably straightforward. Being satisfied with your life even in the absence of some of the trappings of "success." Think again of the example of the individual who is happy in the face of extreme adversity. It is more likely that their own success metric *is* life satisfaction than that it is "achievement."

Focusing on achievement tends to correlate with an overly high degree of focus on the work domain and economic circumstances positively. Again, the reason for this is simple. It is much easier to quantify "success" related to promotions, income, or other measurable deliverables than putting a hierarchical score on the enjoyment of hobbies, pride in parenting style, or satisfaction in a romantic or platonic relationship. Shifting your overall happiness with your "success" to satisfaction in various domains of your life is much more achievable and profitable. Redefining these concepts has a powerful effect. As importantly for the purposes of this book, this shift in thinking opens the way for grit and emotional intelligence to intervene. These tools can prove extremely useful in cultivating life satisfaction.

Finally, it's worth noting that all this is *not* to say that the work you'll do as you read the findings of this book won't lead to an increased drive toward the culmination of achievements. In fact, the opposite is true. Grit and emotional intelligence can undoubtedly help you improve your relationships, obtain career success, and excel in other areas of your life. However, removing some of the pressures of the achievement-driven mindset helps cultivate the most conducive mentality to achievement. Therefore, you should be consciously aware of your perspective as you consider your mindset's directions and how it drifts. Where you find yourself meditating on success or achievement as they relate to your happiness, try to reframe these ideas instead in relation to satisfaction with the individual and individually understood domains of your life. With this, we can dive into Freud's historical understandings of discontentment among the masses.

Theories of Life Satisfaction/Dissatisfaction

While Freud's writings are no longer a standard of modern psychoanalysis or dream interpretation, they provide important historical insight on how modern thought on such topics has developed. Similarly, while life satisfaction theory has emerged and progressed since Freud's time, his work still provides an extremely useful lens to view this topic. To provide a basic summary of his work, Freud views the *death drive* as the antithesis to *eros*, which encompasses concepts like life, love, creativity, satisfaction, and sexuality. This antagonism between eros and the death drive influences behavior. The death drive operates silently in the background, lurking in the unconsciousness to bring an organism back to its primordial inorganic state. Think about the last stand that a person might take when confronted with the realization that life is ending, as seen in Hollywood movies. Freud believed that man is inclined to self-destructive forces that drive unconscious psychic energies that prevent them from fulfilling their destiny and achievement.

The text of *Civilization and Its Discontents* opens as follows:

> The impression forces itself upon one that men measure by false standards, that everyone seeks power, success, riches for himself and admires others who attain them, while undervaluing the truly precious things in life. And yet, in making any general judgment of this kind, one is in danger of forgetting the manifold variety of humanity and its mental life.[37]

This insight is an essential point for our purposes for two reasons. First, Freud has made a very similar point to the one I've been making throughout this book thus far. Achievement, he suggests, is a false standard. There are other elements of life worthy of inclusion in our concept of life satisfaction. And perhaps more importantly, he suggests that human understanding of and definitions of life satisfactions are as broad as humanity itself.

Freud also addresses the widespread difficulty of life and the fact that all individuals must cultivate their own coping mechanisms, which tend to fall into one of three categories.

> Life as we find it is too hard for us; it entails too much pain, too many disappointments, impossible tasks. We cannot do without palliative remedies. We cannot dispense with auxiliary constructions … There are perhaps three of these means: powerful diversions of interest, which lead us to care little about our misery; substitutive gratification, which lessen it; and

---

[37] Sigmund Freud, *Civilization and Its Discontents*, 1930, trans. James Strachey (New York: Norton, 1961), 11.

intoxicating substances, which make us insensitive to it. Something of this kind is indispensable.[38]

This quote provides a powerful opportunity for self-reflection. Which of these three tools do you tend to use when things begin to become too burdensome in any given area of your life? As will be discussed in the following chapters, these potential diversions are key reasons the tools of grit and emotional intelligence are necessary for the first part. For example, grit requires sustained dedication to a drive or goal: not passion in a fleeting sense but over a long period of time. To achieve higher degrees of grit, we must find ways to circumvent Freud's first point about diversion. The process of substituting gratification from achievement to life satisfaction marks a key paradigm shift in our thinking. Suppose we use the metric of overall life satisfaction, allowing for divergences in our satisfaction with different domains of life. In that case, it becomes significantly easier to avoid this type of auxiliary gratification and to shift our focus to the arenas we truly find gratifying.

Regarding happiness, Freud also suggested that it is much more difficult to experience happiness than it is to experience unhappiness. His observations help explain why many self-help books focus on happiness and personal growth instead of despair or misery. When searching the bookshelves, for example, at a brick-and-mortar or online store, you will observe no genres associated with being miserable. The former, he argues, is usually experienced because of a change to circumstances rather than a consistent state of being. He notes too that our experience of happiness is dependent upon our cognitive constitution. This outcome is because unhappiness comes more naturally from, as Freud would have it, three sources: our own body, the external world, and other people. He goes on to suggest,

---

[38] Freud, *Civilization*, 22.

> It is no wonder if, under the pressure of these possibilities to suffering, men are accustomed to moderate their claims to happiness—just as the pleasure principle itself, indeed, under the influence of the external world, changed into the more modest reality principle—if a man thinks himself happy merely to have escaped unhappiness or to have survived his suffering, and if in general the task of avoiding suffering pushes that of obtaining pleasure into the background. Reflection shows that the accomplishment of this task can be attempted along very different paths.[39]

There are two particularly key points to note in this passage. First, it is worth engaging in self-reflection regarding whether your efforts to avoid suffering or those to obtain pleasure are taking more precedence in your thoughts and actions. And similarly, it is worth considering whether your drive to achievement moderates your claims to happiness. Again, this is related to the paradigm shift we need to undertake—as a society, in academic scholarship, and in our own lives—in terms of allowing ourselves to judge our satisfaction with the various domains of our lives outside only the notion of satisfaction as it relates to achievements or perfection in vocational and avocational fields.

Again, while modern interpretations of Freud vary considerably, it is essential to note that his positioning of eros, as opposed to the death drive, is characterized by an understanding of duality. For Freud, these drives operate within the context of our instincts. Thus, even if we disagree with Freud in the exact content of ideas, we can discern resonances with our experiences of duality. This spectrum of drives moves us toward an implicit understanding of satisfaction or dissatisfaction. Given the specific context that shapes reality, these drives can also be responsible for our explicit awareness of such

---

[39] Freud, *Civilization*, 24.

perceptions. It is even possible that we would toggle between an implicit and explicit understanding. Either way, our behaviors are influenced by such dualities.

Freud positions the "instinct of death" in opposition to eros and notes,

> A portion of the instinct is diverted towards the external world and comes to light as an instinct of aggressiveness and destructiveness. In this way the instinct itself could be pressed into the service of Eros, in that the organism was destroying some other thing, whether animate or inanimate, instead of destroying its own self. Conversely, any restriction of this aggressiveness directed outwards would be bound to increase the self-destruction, which is in any case proceeding. At the same time one can suspect from this example that the two kinds of instinct seldom—perhaps never—appear in isolation from each other, but are alloyed with each other in varying and very different proportions and so become unrecognizable to our judgment.[40]

To apply this to our context, rather than considering a death drive and a drive to life, we can consider how we either strive for satisfaction or avoid dissatisfaction. Rather than attempting to create these conditions to experience happiness and life satisfaction, it can be tempting to destroy these conditions that we perceive to be preventing us from achieving such outcomes. While this can be functional if these circumstances are negative, the attempt is still a drive toward destruction rather than one toward furthering passion or perseverance. Thus, alongside the paradigm shift from achievement to satisfaction, the tools of grit and emotional intelligence can be helpful to us. We should use these tools to reconfigure how we think about creating our

---

[40] Freud, *Civilization*, 66.

own version of satisfaction. This deliberate practice can help us focus solely on how we dismantle dissatisfaction in a negative sense.

This insight is important, according to Freud, to avoid the situation in which the aggressiveness "is introjected, internalized ... directed towards his own ego."[41] Freud follows this discussion with one of guilt, and while the discussion in *Civilization and Its Discontents* serves another purpose, this notion serves to indicate another reason why the shift toward life satisfaction as a metric can be imperative. Again, this helps shift us into a more positive space in which we consider what it will take to achieve happiness rather than avoid unhappiness and mitigate the pitfalls of turning this aggression or guilt inward. Indeed, Freud opens his concluding chapter by suggesting that the sense of guilt is "the most important problem in the development of our civilization ... [and] the price we pay for our advance in civilization is a loss of happiness through the heightening of the sense of guilt."[42] In a similar sense, he notes,

> In the process of individual development, as we have said, the main accent falls mostly on the egoistic urge (or the urge towards happiness); while the other urge, which may be described as a "cultural" one, is usually content with the role of imposing restrictions. But in the process of civilization things are different. Here by far the most important thing is the aim of creating a unity out of the individual human beings. It is true that the aim of happiness is still there, but it is pushed into the background. It almost seems as if the creation of a great human community would be most successful if no attention had to be paid to the happiness of the individual.[43]

---

[41] Freud, *Civilization*, 70.
[42] Freud, *Civilization*, 81.
[43] Freud, *Civilization*, 87.

Importantly, while Freud is addressing a broad cultural shift away from the pursuit of happiness or the pleasure principle, we can apply this on a more microcosmic level as well. If we're working—blindly or without sufficient critical thought—toward the goals of a broader entity (e.g., the organization for which we work; societal definitions of a "successful" marriage), it becomes more difficult to pursue individual life satisfaction. This idea is not to suggest that such goals may not align with your personal goals, but considering the instances in which they do and do not match up can help save a significant amount of energy that can be redirected toward their pursuit.

Again—and before moving to other foundational theories on life satisfaction and dissatisfaction—it is important to note that the tools of grit and emotional intelligence are in very good alignment with the pursuit of life satisfaction. They require sustained individual effort and self-reflection on the direction of that effort. They enable us to focus less on guilt and complex challenges; that way, we can cultivate enjoyment as we persevere while focused on the process to overcome challenges. This approach helps us aspire to loftier goals for a more rewarding journey. It is also important to note that this book is not intended to provide only tools for individualistic-minded achievement. Instead, it allows for *individualized* use of grit and emotional intelligence to be used equally and effectively as a vehicle for accomplishments. Some settings that can benefit from using the grit and emotional intelligence constructs include collaborative environments or when working with others, like children, students, or employees.

As will be discussed later in this book, Nietzsche is also an important figure in theoretical conceptions of dissatisfaction; for Nietzsche, this takes the more extreme form of suffering. Schopenhauer influenced some of Nietzsche's early works. To avoid suffering, Schopenhauer believed that it would be best not to have lived at all. His belief on this subject of suffering was in sharp contrast to Nietzsche's philosophy on suffering that developed over the next decade. For Nietzsche, life is most meaningful when we embrace suffering because it provides us with life's true meaning. When we overcome challenges, we sore to new heights of satisfaction. His work partly inspired the groundbreaking work of Austrian psychiatrist and philosopher Victor Frankl, who we discuss shortly.

According to Nietzsche, drives toward satisfaction were not based on unconscious energies conditioning human behavior as described by Freud. For Nietzsche, the conscious energies and conscientious approach to grope incessantly for life's meanings provided the will needed to power through severe challenges. Nietzsche argued that suffering enhanced the human condition because of the journey to overcome suffering. According to the *Stanford Encyclopedia of Philosophy's* precis on the subject,

> Nietzsche's deeper complaints begin from the observation that a morality of compassion centers attention on the problem of suffering, presupposing that suffering is bad as such. Nietzsche resists the hedonistic doctrine that pleasure and pain lie at the basis of all value claims, which would be the most natural way to defend such a presupposition. If he is right that there are other values, independent of consequences for pleasures and pains, that fact raises the possibility that the ultimate value of any particular incidence of suffering could depend on the role it plays in the sufferer's life overall and how it might contribute to those *other* values; in that case, its badness would not follow immediately from the bare fact that it is suffering. Nietzsche builds this idea into a serious argument against the morality of compassion, suggesting that suffering may sometimes promote a person's *growth*, or progress toward excellence.[44]

---

[44] "Friedrich Nietzsche," *Stanford Encyclopedia of Philosophy*, March 17, 2017, https://plato.stanford.edu/entries/nietzsche/.

Significantly, and very similar to our attempt to shift from an achievement-driven mindset to a satisfaction-driven mindset, this indicates that the absence of suffering may not be the most productive goal. While avoiding unnecessary suffering is a useful endeavor, suffering can serve some important purposes. In connection with the idea of grit and emotional intelligence, the view of suffering as a tool can be better understood through self-reflection (i.e., what kind of suffering am I experiencing, and what is its purpose?) and as a way to understand the notion of hard work and perseverance in spite of obstacles somewhat differently.

Influenced by Nietzschean thought, Frankl's reflections on the subject of suffering emerged mainly from his experience of deportation to the Auschwitz concentration camp before being transferred to the Dachau camp in Bavaria. His forced imprisonment facilitated his experience of deep reflection into the human psyche and drove him to understand man's existence better. While Frankl believed suffering could cause some people to move further from the continuum of success, he advocated facing suffering head-on in the hope of achieving transcendence. Frankl's experience in the camps, and the resultant existential frustration, led to his creation of logotherapy, a theory based on a *will to meaning*. According to Frankl, this *will to meaning* allowed people to transcend suffering. At the same time, they searched to find a reason to exist even if they were unsuccessful in life's endeavors. In *Man's Search for Meaning*, Frankl suggests that success should not be the only aim because the more individuals focus on this metric, the more likely they are to miss it.

Similarly, he addressed happiness in the same way. Both concepts relate to his understanding of the choice of attitude as a key to human freedom. "Everything can be taken from a man but … the last of the human freedoms—to choose one's attitude in any given set of circumstances, to choose one's own way."[45] Again, this proposition

---

[45] Victor Frankl, *Man's Search for Meaning* (Boston: Beacon Press, 2006), 104.

aligns very well with the self-reflective component of emotional intelligence and the perseverant tools of grit. If we can harness these tools, it becomes much more likely that we will be able to choose our own attitude and, according to Frankl, use this to move more entirely toward a heightened experience of life satisfaction.

Like Angela Duckworth, Frankl addresses drive and perseverance in connection with the drive toward developing and furthering life satisfaction. Frankl noted, "Logotherapy ... considers man as a being whose main concern consists in fulfilling a meaning and in actualizing values, rather than in the mere gratification and satisfaction of drives and instincts."[46] Even more strikingly—and bringing Duckworth into conversation with Nietzsche by way of Frankl—he noted that "what man actually needs is not a tensionless state but the striving and struggling for some goal worthy of him. What he needs is not the discharge of tension at any cost, but the call of a potential meaning waiting to be fulfilled by him."[47] This perspective blends a somewhat less severe version of Nietzsche's positive view on the potential of suffering (framing it as tension rather than suffering as such), with Duckworth's focus on persevering toward the object of one's passion, in spite of obstacles. Importantly, it is key that all such theories focus on this pursuit not as a negative to be overcome and forgotten about but as something that can exist in conjunction with life satisfaction. And again, the shift from a focus on achievement to one of satisfaction is a key step on this journey from viewing suffering/tension/obstacles/challenges as inherently negative but as things that can be addressed through perseverance and that can coexist with the experience of life satisfaction.

Finally, on the overall understanding of life satisfaction, Frankl noted,

> It did not really matter what we expected from life, but what life expected from us. We needed to stop asking

---

[46] Frankl, *Man's Search*, 164.
[47] Frankl., Man's Search, 166.

about the meaning of life, and instead to think of ourselves as those who were being questioned by life—daily and hourly. Our answer must consist, not in talk ad meditation, but in right action and in right conduct. Life ultimately means taking the responsibility to find the right answer to its problems and to fulfill the tasks which it constantly sets for each individual.[48]

While this section addresses these theories very briefly compared to their import in the field of philosophy, and while they differ significantly in their origins and conclusion, they serve to indicate some significant points that relate to our overall project in this book. First, they can all be viewed as aligning with the shift from focusing on achievement to life satisfaction as a metric. From Freud's notion of civilization as impeding the drive toward happiness and instilling guilt to Frankl's proposition that we should consider ourselves questioned by life on a daily basis rather than achieving an overall understanding of the meaning of life, these historical understandings of dissatisfaction all seem to agree with the idea that there is more to a satisfying life than there is to achievement. They therefore acknowledge that it is a key and complex pursuit.

Suppose we can consider our relative levels of life satisfaction accurately even though they can change across time and differ across domains of life. In this case, we can harness suffering and tension as a vehicle rather than viewing it as inherently and inescapably negative. We can be happy even in the absence of the end-point achievements for which we strive. This direction is key in maintaining the perseverance needed to achieve them; if we cultivate happiness at the steps along the way to our goals, we are much more likely to continue in their pursuit. Further, these different theories align well with this book's focus on the emotional intelligence tool of self-reflection. Again, suppose one of these theories resonates with you more than another. In that case, I encourage you to consider your experience concerning that theory.

---

[48] Frankl, *Man's Search*, 122.

Once evaluated, you can move toward understanding how you are currently experiencing life dissatisfaction or satisfaction. Perhaps this understanding will provide you with a prospective understanding of how you'd like to experience it. Before moving to our discussion of the effects of life dissatisfaction, the following section provides some more recent research—in the field of positive psychology rather than philosophy—on how to understand life satisfaction.

More recently, a foundational study on the concept of life satisfaction, the work by Lykken and Tellegen, involved coining the term "set point" to clarify the individual differences in happiness levels that do not seem to correlate to demographic factors. Noting that "although people adapt surprisingly quickly to both good news and bad, the set-point around which happiness varies from time to time apparently differs from one person to another,"[49] the authors surveyed 2,310 twins regarding their levels of life satisfaction. The authors suggested that genetics and experiences appear to have similar roles in terms of their contributions to life satisfaction. They concluded that well-being and life satisfaction largely depend on chance (both genetic and experiential experiences). Science now knows that people with the short version of the 5-HTTLPR (a neurotransmitter serotonin transporter gene) are more reactive to stressful environments. They are more likely to be depressed and more prone to anxiety and elevated cortisol levels if the environment is overly stressful. Although genetics matter, environmental conditions do as well. Some people appear more genetically wired for resiliency and happiness if they have the longer gene version. This finding might explain why some leaders are more resilient and effective given extreme conditions. Perhaps, this finding could shed insight into Winston Churchill's effective leadership style during World War II. Compared to Neville Chamberlain's inept Munich agreement that annexed Czechoslovakia, he was an astute political leader. We should think about these points when reflecting

---

[49] David Lykken and Auke Tellegen, "Happiness Is a Stochastic Phenomenon," *Psychological Science* 7, no. 3 (1996): 186.

on nature and nurture roles. In short, genetics matter as much as environmental conditions. The article ended with the oft-quoted axiom "It may be that trying to be happier is as futile as trying to be taller and therefore is counterproductive."[50] While pithy, this quote may be—surprisingly—more disheartening than the material on suffering offered by Nietzsche. What is important to take from this study is not the idea that happiness cannot be achieved. Instead, individuals have different predispositions for how they experience it. Emotional intelligence tools can help address this issue by understanding how we currently undergo life satisfaction. It also helps us know how we aim to experience it while working to alter our satisfaction in life.

Somewhat more encouragingly, Headey and Muffels addressed the notion of the set-point theory of life satisfaction. They asserted that life satisfaction remains stable over time with brief situational alterations with a view that medium-term life satisfaction might replace. Their viewpoint implies that the "good" and "bad" times people experience can be more extended. More specifically, the researchers noted that people tend to experience multiple-year periods where their level of life satisfaction rises above or decreases below their overall twenty-year mean. They also tested for specific domains that improve life satisfaction. These domains include the existence of a positive feedback loop between exercise and enhanced life satisfaction. These findings were similar to the earlier results of active social participation and the overall state of a person's health. Thus, a new model of medium-term change is needed. In addition, researchers noted that future studies should account for the long-term changes that occur throughout the life span because it influences life satisfaction.

Addressing the construct of life satisfaction and the emergence of positive psychology as a field, Pavot and Diener noted that "among the constituent components of SWB [subjective well-being], life satisfaction has been identified as a distinct construct representing a cognitive and

---

[50] Lykken and Tellegen, "Happiness," 189.

global evaluation of the quality of one's life as a whole."[51] The broader concept of subjective well-being includes negative effect and positive effect as well as life satisfaction. The researcher's summary provided insight into the satisfaction component on life scale (SWLS) regarding its uses and efficacy. Importantly, Pavot and Diener noted that personality traits, such as extraversion, neuroticism, life events, and circumstances, tend to affect life satisfaction. Since personality traits and various life domains affect life satisfaction, it provides an "integrated judgment of how a person's life as a whole is going."[52] Assessing the SWLS, the authors considered studies that used the scale in several categories for cross-culturally relevant studies. Data from diverse populations were included, including clinical and counseling issues and health-related studies. They determined the findings to be reliable and valid across domains.

Whether from longstanding philosophy or more contemporary positive psychology, I hope that these views on life satisfaction or dissatisfaction are useful in framing the need for this book. Further, they should help clarify why the shift from a focus on achievement to one more centered on the idea of life satisfaction is necessary.

The Effects of Life Dissatisfaction

Perhaps the most obvious and severe effect of life dissatisfaction is the incidence of depression and suicide outcomes. Several studies have shown a correlation between depression outcomes and reported life satisfaction.[53] Depression is a health condition that requires

---

[51] William Pavot and Ed Diener, "The Satisfaction with Life Scale and the Emerging Construct of Life Satisfaction," *The Journal of Positive Psychology* 3, no. 2 (2008): 137.
[52] Pavot and Diener, "Satisfaction with Life Scale," 140.
[53] Manfred E. Beutel et al., "Life Satisfaction, Anxiety, Depression and Resilience across the Life Span of Men," *The Aging Male* 13, no. 1 (2010): 32–39; Sevgi Guney, Temel Kalafat, and Murat Boysan, "Dimensions of Mental Health: Life Satisfaction, Anxiety and Depression: A Preventive Mental Health Study in Ankara University Students Population," *Procedia-Social and Behavioral Sciences* 2, no. 2 (2010): 1210–1213; Viren Swami et al., "General Health Mediates the Relationship between Loneliness, Life Satisfaction and Depression," *Social Psychiatry and Psychiatric Epidemiology* 42, no. 2 (2007): 161–166.

psychological or medical intervention. We should treat mental illness with the same gravitas as any physical ailment. As most studies addressed in the previous section showed, life satisfaction is more closely related to a mindset that can change over time. My intention is not to suggest that depression can be addressed in the same way as alterations to your reported life satisfaction can be changed. Clinical depression requires additional intervention. My purpose is also not to suggest that low life satisfaction levels are the main, and certainly not the only, causes of depression. What I am saying about this subject is that one key effect of negative life satisfaction can be depression. Suppose you are currently experiencing lower than desired levels of life satisfaction in the absence of depression symptoms. In that case, this is an important reason to take any possible actions to improve life satisfaction and reduce life dissatisfaction across domains of life.

While this field is too broad to precis here, it is worth noting that lower levels of life satisfaction positively correlate with decreased productivity and higher instances of burnout. In a vocational arena, lower levels of job satisfaction correlate positively with higher turnover rates and lower levels of work-life balance. In a relational arena, life satisfaction correlates positively with the ability to engage in caregiving, parenting, or teaching behaviors without experiencing complete burnout. I would suggest, as well, that declining life satisfaction in one area of life can negatively impact that in other areas of life. While it is important to conceive of these separately as related to their own domains, it is also the case that they can spill over into one another. Conversely, improvements to one area of life satisfaction can have a positive effect—as if by osmosis—on others.

Most importantly—and the reason this section is brief—it is imperative to engage in self-reflection to understand your own experience of life satisfaction and dissatisfaction. Once you have a clear understanding of your state of mind, you can develop a plan for how you may want to go about addressing or altering it. The following questions are designed to spark reflection on your levels of satisfaction or dissatisfaction and how they're affecting you:

1. How would you rate your satisfaction with your relational life (romantic relationships, friendships, parent-child relationships, other familial relationships, relationships with colleagues) on a scale from 1 to 100?
2. How would you rate your satisfaction with your work-life (whether vocational, educational, or other—including work-life balance) on a scale from 1 to 100?
3. How would you rate your satisfaction with the areas of life that are unrelated to your responsibilities (self-care, hobbies, and other pursuits) on a scale from 1 to 100?

For each of these areas:

1. How does this satisfaction level affect you emotionally and with your physical and mental health?
2. How does this satisfaction level affect your view of life as successful or unsuccessful in this domain?
3. How does this satisfaction level affect how you tend to challenges or obstacles in this domain of life?

While this section is brief, there will be many more opportunities for self-reflection in the later chapters of this book. My intention with this chapter is to provide different theoretical, academic, and personal impetuses for thought. The purpose is to enable you to begin a process of self-reflection to understand yourself. Then you can work toward making alterations to various parts of your life with the end goal of improving your satisfaction in life as necessary.

CHAPTER 3

My Story

The purpose of this chapter is to indicate my expertise, both personal and professional, on this subject. This chapter's chief goal is to provide you with more insight on why I decided to conduct a novel study on grit and life satisfaction in the first place. I present a personal story of my journey from a life of dissatisfaction to satisfaction to accomplish this objective. I also provide many examples that align with the preceding theoretical and academic material on this subject to help bring the concepts included therein to life. Finally, after reading my story, I hope you feel more empowered to undertake the challenging but immeasurably rewarding work of self-reflection on this subject.

This section is a psychological autobiography written as a monologue of myself. Sometimes it may appear to function as a psychological autopsy because of the deep reflective thought associated with the psyche that gave me a cathartic release. Nevertheless, this transparent approach to understanding myself through a psychological lens presents the reader with a rich account of my development from adolescence to adulthood. I thought long and hard about the various themes written from a cerebral perspective removed from emotion and how they fit into the psychological framework of this book.

As stated at the outset of this chapter, one purpose of presenting my personal story in this chapter is to encourage you in your process of self-reflection. You will learn to create space for individual narratives within the academic material and practical recommendations that compose the majority of this text. Afterward, you will move to the in-depth material on my study and—in part 2—my synthesis of other scholarship and practical recommendations as a result. The purpose of this section is to provide you with a deeper understanding of how I became interested in this subject and why I became an expert on it. My expertise in this topic, in other words, is both personal and professional. I have found grit and emotional intelligence tools to be integral to my experience in both capacities. As such, this section includes material both on my story itself and on the scholarly and philosophical materials that I view as relating most directly to it.

My experience with external impediments to life satisfaction began early, as kindergarten teachers and administration labeled me mentally challenged. At this time, they explained to my parents that I must be mentally retarded. Without additional explanation or diagnoses, the phrase "mentally retarded" was used constantly by teachers and school administrators when they explained their observations of me. While cognitively delayed, I remember being consistently self-aware of the individual differences between my twin sister and me. Although we never thought much about the issues that could surface later in life due to improperly labeling me. They would prove to be more challenging to run from than running an entire marathon with no training. The visceral effects of these derogatory labels and statements had unforeseen consequences for the course of my future, and I am still grappling with its aftermath.

This debilitating and embarrassing label felt permanent, and it would prove to be a profound hindrance to my future success. Labeling any child as mentally retarded causes many cognitive challenges throughout the life span. Indeed, based on my personal experience with it, I am thankful for the declassification of this label by the American Psychiatric Association. The *Diagnostic and Statistical Manual of Mental Disorders (DSM-5)* replaced this label with "intellectual disabilities" to explain a range of intellectual developmental disorders in its 2013 edition.[54] Any disability labeled improperly—as this one was—could exaggerate the developmental issues the child faces. This improper label could delay their cognitive growth and produce the unintended consequence of limiting their success outcomes. More specifically, intellectual development disorders can cause lower levels of self-esteem that influence a child's confidence while fostering pathological insecurities within their minds psyche. This phenomenon exacerbates the situation even further when they are assigned improper appellatives as I was.

Brain Plasticity, Cognitive Development, and Learned Helplessness

The effects of low self-esteem and low confidence are contributing factors that influence learned helplessness. Another factor affecting cognition is an openness to new experiences. Learned helplessness restricts the child's movement and stifles their curiosity, causing them to avoid novel experiences. Stressful conditions in a child's life could teach them to feel helpless because of the repeated inability to control or escape from an overwhelming situation.[55] This inability to cope with stressful conditions created an atmosphere of failure that led to depression.

Nevertheless, giving up on a task or life is not a human phenomenon. Animals learn to be helpless too, if stressful conditions remove any

---

[54] American Psychiatric Association, *Diagnostic and Statistical Manual of Mental Disorders: DSM-5* (Arlington, VA: American Psychiatric Association, 2013).
[55] Gregory J. Feist and Erica L. Rosenberg, *Psychology: Perspectives and Connections* (McGraw-Hill: New York, 2018), 584.

sense of control and prevent them from escaping from a cage. The learned helplessness of animals is now part of a classic experiment that placed a metal floor in a cage that shocked the animal at various points. After each successful shock, the animal learned helplessness and gave up trying to escape. Their behavior suggested that their minds must have felt defeated. Being in control and having the ability and means to run from stressful conditions takes ingenuity that is solution based for animals and humans.[56]

As these constructs begin to take root in the child's psyche, they can have a paralyzing effect on their behavior, contributing to the likelihood of depression. For example, my intellectual disabilities restricted my movements in the classroom and from engaging in activities with other children, which could have presented new opportunities for growth and learning. Learning gains were meager at best and more challenging to acquire when I could not move around much. I learned to be reactive rather than to initiate action because I felt helpless. Whether self-induced or applied by leadership or parents, these restrictions make understanding key concepts—like grit and emotional intelligence—and skills more difficult. If environments are overly restricted, depression could take residence in the child's mind, as it did in mine. A combination of lower degrees of grit and emotional intelligence partly explains why such children cannot overcome obstacles and setbacks while maintaining a constant interest in activities. These social deficiencies make it more difficult for the child to evaluate their emotions appropriately and other people's emotions. It also means that the child cannot adapt their feelings based on social cues to social context. These skills are contextual, and if children lack these skills, then their effort is thwarted. Suppose children cannot develop higher degrees of grit and emotional intelligence. In that case, opportunities

---

[56] Stephen F. Maier and Martin E. P. Seligman, "Learned Helplessness at Fifty: Insights from Neuroscience," *Psychological Review* 123, no. 4 (2016): 349. http://dx.doi.org/10.1037/rev0000033.

to nurture these basic constructs become limited, and satisfaction levels suffer throughout their life span.

If the child is isolated from play and inclusive environments for long periods, they may have fewer opportunities to develop grit and emotional intelligence. Sensing stimuli externally is the beginning of knowledge. However, long periods of sensory deprivation dull the senses in the human brain. We can observe the effects of a depressed brain by examining brain scans of children from a Romanian orphanage.[57] Brain scans revealed a curious finding of how the brain reacts to sensory deprivation and stimulation differently. Scientists relied upon a Positron Emission Tomography (PET) scan to measure brain activity. This innovative technology could look at the brain in real time to observe which of its four constitutional parts reacted to external stimuli or its lack. The human brain's metabolic activity and blood flow could be traced and measured after a radioactive tracer mapped its path during a given task or not.

The senses can be heightened or dulled based on the environments that children occupy. We know that satisfaction scores are lower for depressed people. Researchers demonstrated that children in an unresponsive and unexciting environment showed more depressed brain activity than children growing up in a stimulating environment.[58] Children's social structures should be predictable. They should have opportunities to engage in novel experiences with other children and various activities to stimulate the brain to develop correctly. Suppose the brain doesn't develop normally. What then? Children's brains develop and react to stressful environments that shape their thinking and alter their behavior. In that case, the children may become more prone to depression and become more emotionally despondent. It's a profound misunderstanding to think that emotionally despondent children cannot engage in meaningful activities. At first glance, this might hold, but they need new experiences to activate them into action

---

[57] J. W. Santrock, *Life-span Development*, 17th ed. (New York: McGraw-Hill, 2015), 110.
[58] J. W. Santrock, *Life-span Development*, 17th ed. (New York: McGraw-Hill, 2015).

to overcome their melancholy. The lack of a meaningful context means they are more likely to experience lower satisfaction levels in their lives.

The Romanian orphanage study is of particular importance to me. As a child, I was not in the most engaging or desirable of environments. My siblings were often invited to events by other children and therefore had more opportunities than I did to play. As a result, they had more experiences that nurtured the cognitive development that comes with those situations. My parents observed and responded to these social deficits. They provided me with a warm, authoritative style. This parenting style provided a reliable, respectful, and loving environment with the proper structure that made me feel comfortable. They reacted by providing me with tutors and private lessons to help me socially and academically, but I resisted. Once I decided to close myself off from others, it was never easy to ask for help again.

As an adult, I still resist asking people for help when needed. My aversion to accepting assistance from people was rooted in my early adolescence when I felt rejected by my peers. I often wonder how my brain developed in an unstimulating and unresponsive environment that limited me socially. And how it might have developed if I had instead had more opportunity to adapt to my surroundings. I will never know for sure, but I suspect that a brain scan might have revealed mine as a depressed brain, similar to those of the children in the orphanage. It is also plausible that my Broca's and Wernicke's areas were underdeveloped since my speech and listening skills were lacking. My melancholy during adolescence and my inability to use productive speech and comprehend language quickly suggest that these areas of my brain were immature.

The Romanian orphanage study prompted researchers to ask a fundamental question about the brain's ability to develop normally. Could the depressed brain eventually show evidence of higher brain activity? Did the brain show evidence of neuroplasticity? We turn to another landmark study to examine these questions to determine whether the brain's capacity to change is possible. The research revealed important information and data about the brain's plasticity after scientists observed the brain's resiliency to changes after removing the left hemisphere of a seven-year-old. Michael Rehbein started experiencing approximately four hundred seizures daily in his left hemisphere. Although the left hemisphere is essential for language processing and comprehension, surgeons removed Michael's left hemisphere to stop the seizures. Unfortunately, removing this hemisphere meant that he would not have the needed cortical areas for language processing. As a result, communicating with people would be virtually impossible.

The removal of the left hemisphere of the brain presented a curious finding to researchers. The right hemisphere of Michael's brain recognized and responded to the language deficits that emerged after removing the left hemisphere. The right hemisphere started to reorganize. It began to rewire neural pathways to develop new connections with cortical areas associated with this region of the hemisphere. Broca's and Wernicke's areas are language areas responsible for speech production and speech comprehension, respectively. In Michael's case, areas in the opposite hemisphere replaced these lateralized areas. Researchers believe that repeated experiences with language acquisition can lead to the brain's rewiring of neural pathways in specific cortical regions of the opposite hemisphere. It appears that the right hemisphere could rewire itself for language because it is biologically predisposed to do so through a complex network of neurons. Nerve cells migrate to other regions of the brain to reorganize lost functions. Synchronization of these neurons allows for a complex and intricate network of neurons to make synaptic connections with adjacent neurons. These connections become strengthened by repeated experiences of external stimuli. The association areas of the cerebral cortex helped rewire some of these deficits with other areas to replace the functions of speech production and comprehension associated with language processing. Although language recovery takes years to process, acquiring these lost skills after surgery is possible. Another curious finding is that the right hemisphere used far more cortical space to replace the language lost after removing the left hemisphere. Although not exclusive to the left hemisphere, this finding suggested the lateralization of language acquisition. Since the brain can rewire itself after an anatomical hemispherectomy, then a contextual change to a more engaging environment could support the brain's plasticity for some people. These observations suggested that the brain is flexible, malleable, and resilient because of repeated experiences.

The plasticity of Michael Rehbein's brain presented two curious findings. First, the brain's left hemisphere specializes in language processing and comprehension more so than the right hemisphere. Second, the brain is more resilient than previously thought, and it can rewire neural pathways based on repeated experiences. The brain seeks to repair adjacent cortical areas, as seen with some types of cerebral hemorrhages. Of course, the severity of the stroke associated with cortical lesions to the brain influences the likelihood of recovery. Still, it suggests that the recovery of a lost skill or function is possible. However, rewiring brain areas after a hemispherectomy could take many years for adequate healing. Although it might take years for the brain to rewire itself, the brain's dramatic attempt to allocate necessary cortical resources to the other hemisphere for language is impressive.

Processing speech and language is an evolutionary design that helps people adapt to their surroundings and communicate for social reasons. These findings suggest that the brain is malleable and flexible. While this plasticity can prove positive—as it did in Michael's case—the opposite outcome can also occur. Repeated negative experiences can rewire and depress the brain due to persistent experiences in an unresponsive and unstimulating environment. Why does this matter? In my experience, the repeated labeling of mental retardation in the lackluster school environments restricted extracurricular opportunities for me to play and socialize with other children. It's plausible that my early childhood experiences rewired my brain's neural pathways and changed my experiences so that this lack of connection and feeling of inferiority became the norm.

A lack of opportunities restricts children from properly assessing their own and other people's emotions because they are not interacting with people frequently. Social connections and context make the difference between the child functioning properly or not. Having few social interactions can cause a child to remain on the fringe of their society, with few incentives and opportunities to enhance their existence. Cognition, behavior, and environment are three elements critical to developing the social skills needed while learning to adapt to external stimuli in the environment. Eventually, the gap associated with these vital skills becomes so tremendous and noticeable that the helplessness learned early in childhood is further reinforced throughout the life span. Every rejection or experience of exclusion manifests feelings of inadequacy.

When I was a child, I never knew how to persevere through complex challenges. Once confronted with an obstacle, I was unable to adapt to changed circumstances during primary education. This trend continued through my secondary education. My inability to adjust contextually to life's significant events was concerning. It caused me to retreat from a challenge and forfeit any attempt to avoid further social humiliation that resulted from me prattling on with an occasional faux pas. We know how unforgiving children can be when they observe a child embarrassing themselves with an inappropriate remark in any situation. They typically poke fun at the child before they ignore the child altogether. Once ostracized from social events, the struggle to regain acceptance is a tough uphill battle for any child. Although these observations are from my own subjective experiences during childhood, adolescence, and emerging adulthood, it is only now, as a psychologist, that I can adequately articulate the psychological influence that a cognitive label and resultant isolation had on my development.

Education System Problems

Returning to my story, these initial observations from teachers and administration remained in place until I reached third grade. At that time, I was in an inclusive classroom that included students labeled as "gifted." I remember experiencing minimal interaction with these students because I was slow in my cognitive processing. The minimum interaction with other students was hurtful and caused me to feel like an outsider.

Nevertheless, during this grade, I remember taking a standardized mathematics test. This test measured the individual differences associated with mathematics districtwide. Although many students earned satisfactory scores, my results were perfect. Administrators were surprised by my test results. They made it clear to my parents that I scored the highest in the school. Rather than being praised, they accused me of academic dishonesty. How could a cognitively delayed student outperform every student, including the gifted students? Why was it so difficult to believe that a cognitively delayed student couldn't achieve a perfect score? These and similar questions seemed to puzzle administrators and teachers. They shared some of these viewpoints with my parents after accusing me of dishonesty.

After the academic inquisition, the administrators ordered a battery of tests to screen me for disabilities. These cognitive assessments revealed my learning disabilities in more detail. The test reported that I had dyslexia and dysgraphia but not dyscalculia. At this point, the test battery I received also determined that I had an auditory processing deficit that prevented me from understanding sounds and integrating vowels and consonants. Wernicke's area is responsible for language comprehension. In that case, it reasons that this area of my left temporal lobe was immature. This inability to integrate vowels and consonants makes learning a foreign language more difficult for any child or adult. It also makes communication in your native tongue challenging. Constantly asking people to repeat their last comment because I didn't process the phoneme correctly becomes an annoyance to all involved in the conversation. To cope with this listening deficit, I stayed quiet.

While I still experience this problem as an adult, I have learned to mask it well. I also remember the school I attended as deeply unhelpful in diagnosing and accommodating my different abilities. The teachers and administrators recommended that I repeat the same grade every year since I continually underperformed compared to the other students. These observations from teachers meant that I could not learn at the same speed as my twin sister and the other students in my classrooms who were not learning impaired. At this point in my education, I refused homework partly because I was tired of the labels and angry at my teachers' belittling. However, this constant criticism of my skills actually affected me physically, academically, and intellectually.

Years later, I almost failed high school but was pushed through by the administration. As an adult, I have often wondered how this could happen. Moving me through the system provided me with a social and academic disadvantage. Each successive grade level required foundational material from the previous grade level. These deficits in my academic skills became more apparent as I struggled to keep pace with course material in the successive grade. Eventually, I would graduate from high school, but I was unprepared for college and the real world. The obsession with graduation rates is not a new phenomenon. Graduation rates refer to the percentage of the student population that graduates based on the dropout denominator. As an educator, I realize the administrators who pushed me through high school were just as concerned with graduation rates as current administrators are. This obsession with graduation rates has led to a very high percentage of students graduating from high school.

The "Case against Zero" and Other Systemic Issues with Education

Although schools continue to recruit highly qualified teachers, they often find new teachers with temporary teaching certificates. They usually have up to a year to satisfy state requirements, and poorer districts are more likely to invite this practice. Sharon Wynne noted, "The significance of this responsibility can be seen in the current national research that shows that of all high school graduates, only about 72% enrolled as a freshman. The drop-out rate for high school students is estimated to be around 20–30%."[59]

However, it is worth asking, "Is it normal for schools to have graduation rates at or over 95 percent every year? What policies explain this phenomenon? Is federal and state funding linked to graduation rates? If so, how and how are these scores procured? Is it possible to improve the graduation rates by moving a portion of the troubled student enrollment to other schools to meet the school or district's objective? If so, what written procedures explain this process? Were any grading curves enacted at the state and district level to improve these metrics on a standardized test to reduce the number of failures? What percentage of students were removed from the enrollment rosters to improve these metrics? Suppose the graduation rate in some districts is genuinely over the ninetieth percentile. Why don't we have more productive students who possess the skills and talent to function correctly in life? Why are we not seeing more geniuses emerging from our schools?" These questions are rhetorical, intended to encourage the reader to contemplate some statistics that appear as anomalies.

In my view, we should take a quantitative approach to these questions before examining qualitative data for understanding. Statistical anomalies need an explanation with a particular reference point in mind. We should impugn the integrity of any data that

---

[59] Sharon A. Wynne, *Highly Qualified Teachers: Florida Educational Leadership Examination* (Melrose: XAMonline, Inc., 2018), 83.

appears as an outlier. For example, suppose a salesperson is an outlier in his department. He produces a significantly higher commission amount that seems to be out of alignment with other seasoned sales representatives. Should we assume he is the best salesperson, or could there be another explanation for the sales volume being out of variance to others in the department? These are reasonable questions to ask as a midlevel manager.

Statistical anomalies need further investigation to understand the individual's behavior or the organization that employs him. For example, an internal audit of his production could reveal commission malfeasance. It is also possible that he might be more talented than his associates. They might discover that he has a significant number of referrals from his sphere of influence. He might even work over seventy-five hours weekly compared to his peers, who work fewer than forty-five hours. Nevertheless, a quantitative approach to the outlier's production led to valid explanations qualitatively.

We should approach the national graduation rates in school districts with the same quantitative and qualitative methods used in private industries. The data should also reveal the individual differences within the student population. Suppose we approach student performance through a skeptical lens. In that case, we would be better able to identify the deficits of each student. The goal should not be to move them through the system unless they have foundational knowledge that improves areas of weaknesses. Think how much more productive a student would be if we could improve their blind spots rather than focusing only on their strengths. It is not practical for a society to focus simply on achieving the best graduation rates possible without providing students the support they need. We should never lose sight of the forest because of our unwillingness to see beyond the trees. A universal plan and practice nationwide could help eliminate some of these academic confounds that cloud the data to assess individual differences and learning gains more appropriately.

Many of the teachers in my school district have embraced a new ideology in recent years. It's apparent to me that this new philosophy could artificially improve graduation rates. And this new belief could prevent students from developing adequate degrees of grit and emotional knowledge needed to compete in a changing world. This philosophy emerged four years ago during professional development training. "The case against zero" was introduced to teachers as an educational philosophy.[60] To understand this new philosophy, we must first explain it before asking why teachers embrace it. The premise of this practice gives a student a 50 percent grade for work they did not complete instead of a zero. It also provides a student with a 50 percent or better regardless of how poorly they do on an exam. This idea advocated that this grading practice gave students hope to pass, especially those in the lowest tiers. They argued that a grade of zero is unfair because there is only a 10 percent difference between the letter grades, such as A, B, C, and D. A 60 percent difference exists between zero and the lowest passing grade. Rather than a normal distribution of grades, data points would appear asymmetrical with a skewed right tail.

Practices like the *case against zero* would cause a business to go out of business, yet we use them all the time in the public school system. Although this philosophy helps students pass courses, does it teach students how to be resilient and gritty and succeed in life? How do we teach students to be resilient and gritty when this policy suggests that life is easy and requires less work for success? Does this policy positively influence graduation rates? As the graduation rate increases nationally, we should expect an increase in students enrolling in remedial English and mathematics classes as freshmen in college unless colleges lower their standards. I am no longer mealymouthed about my observations. My professional view is that the case against zero is the antithesis to developing grit and emotional knowledge.

---

[60] "Teachers Defend 'No-Zero' Grading Policy," *WPTV News*, September 26, 2018, <https://www.youtube.com/watch?v=I4mXsbpE5nA>.

A prudent pedagogy is vitally essential to the academic health of our institutions for students to develop the right skills to compete and thrive in the twenty-first century. The recent COVID-19 pandemic raises several concerns related to student success. First, student attendance and engagement appear to be lower than they were before the COVID-19 period. Second, many students' shifting from campus to virtual learning platforms sounded alarm bells to this year's graduation rates. Third, a liberal grading policy that replaced zeros with 50 percent or better scores has made its way back to professional learning communities. To be fair and even understanding to administrators and teachers that endorsed this philosophy, they are searching for viable solutions to a challenging problem about the level of motivation that aligns with graduation rates. I believe teachers' hearts are in the right place, but I fear that the case against zero could erode a culture of meritocracy. Missing the mark is a sin against the integrity of the education system. When we neglect to do what is right, it is a sin of omission. Educators, therefore, must adhere to a superlative system of education that goes beyond state standards. Fourth, educators must maintain a higher philosophical reasoning level that improves pedagogical awareness and student accountability. Finally, criteria grounded in ethics make it flexible yet stern enough to help students develop the skills needed to be grittier and more emotionally knowledgeable. Grit and emotional intelligence can lead to a healthier mind equipped for all eventualities. The absence of these skills could be harmful to students' future employment prospects and life satisfaction.

We should address this academic contagion before it becomes much more challenging to control. If left unrestrained, this contagion has the potential to become an academic pandemic. Acts that encourage academic merit could replace practices that discourage and demotivate effort among students and teachers. For example, teachers' relaxed approach to grading appears in their personal and professional achievements alongside a mutual indifference to learning. In short, this practice can make teachers lazy—a behavior they learned from their students.

Thorndike's law of effect states that "the consequences of a behavior increasing (decreasing) the likelihood that the behavior will be repeated."[61] Students are great manipulators who constantly try to negotiate their work with teachers based on their learning preferences, which are not usually productive. They are strategic opportunists if not managed. They know how to exploit systems and policies to their advantage. For example, when they realize that other students benefit from a liberal grading policy designed to promote a perception of equity, they leap into action as a unified force.

Albert Bandura's social learning theory describes how observational learning can reinforce behaviors by modeling or imitating other people's behaviors.[62] We are conditioning students to ignore difficult assignments every time we give them half the grade for work not earned. What would happen to students' motivation and overall performance if all teachers adhered to a universal rule that opposed the case against zero? Students might then realize that teachers are serious about them doing their work and that their preferred excuses are, in fact, no excuse for failing to complete their assignments.

The culture of grit that teachers tried to promote decayed like an old, withered tree lacking the nourishment that the soil and the sun once provided. Educators should be mindful that grit is the aggregate of habits, not its absence. Practices are not always enjoyable, yet we all have them. Some of these habits foster undesirable behaviors, such as not completing a task or assignment or giving up prematurely. These unwanted behaviors make it more challenging to measure performance against an academic yardstick. And some practices help us develop skills with much-needed efforts, such as ability, passion, and hard work. These practices can help us shun complacency so we too can become

---

[61] Gregory J. Feist and Erica L. Rosenberg. *Psychology: Perspectives and Connections* (New York: McGraw-Hill, 2018), 305.
[62] Feist and Rosenberg, *Psychology*, 320.

paragons in our field of study. This no-zero practice could develop into a philosophy that teaches kids that they only need to complete half the work to have an easy life. Although this strategy is most likely unwritten in some school districts, it appears to be embraced by many students and teachers. However, the more equipped you are to deal with life's biggest challenges, the more fulfilled you are.

Educators recognize that the amount of information required to learn and teach has increased exponentially over several decades. The enormous amount of material is a burden for both teachers and students. Regular conversations with teachers have informed me that most teachers are frustrated with the material needed to cover the course curriculum. I never heard a single teacher say that they have enough time to cover the course material in the time frame given. Administrators and teachers addressed these concerns by collaborating with staff to streamline material and chunk valuable information for students. Unfortunately, this practice led to more students ignoring reading assignments in place of a study guide and worksheet with the answers. This approach to chunk information into digestible pieces requires more time and effort and a great deal of planning by the teacher, nevertheless most students prefer it. However, the amount of time that a teacher needs to do their job effectively is not adequate. Time is a scarce resource with which teachers struggle because many unknown variables occur during a typical school day.

As a result, many effective teachers work outside their contracts to plan for the next school day. In contrast, many of them work several jobs to earn additional income to earn a livable wage because their earnings are depressed. Thus, time and planning become problematic for many teachers who are spread thin and exhausted from their many responsibilities. Suppose the state doesn't want to solve the problem associated with teachers' wages because of the institutional indifference to their social life. In that case, a temporary moratorium of the state's plenary powers could provide a small window of opportunity for the US Department of Education to present a wage solution. This change in teacher compensation would attract and encourage the next generation of instructors responsible for influencing the next generation of minds.

The school budget is partly determined and controlled by the Consumer Price Index to take into account inflation. Schools are budgeted with more funds to cover operating expenses related to expenditures because of this index. Teachers' low wages should always keep pace with inflation to minimize their economic struggles. This index could be a viable solution to teacher wages. I cannot recall when I overheard a student say that they can't wait until they graduate from a university. That way, they can work multiple jobs simultaneously. This type of utterance would appear mad to a sane person, yet this is the reality of many teachers who hold advanced degrees. Many teachers cannot afford homes in their district unless they have more than one income and employer. The constant struggle for scarce resources caused them to feel dissatisfied. There needs to be a balance between work and nonwork activities. When teachers work multiple jobs to make ends meet, their well-being and satisfaction levels suffer significantly, along with their performance and health. In short, a national discussion about the inequitable nature of wages should be a priority for stakeholders. It's a systemic problem that is inherent in the education system.

Wage issues for teachers, not the highly paid district administrators, need immediate redress. A good starting point to solve this problem is an equitable compensation plan for education reform that can attract students to the profession. I often hear teachers say it's all about the kids, and they should come first. However, teachers' interests should go before the students. A hungry person will remain hungry until they have their fill. They are not much use to anyone else until they reach satiety. Suppose teachers' economic needs aren't satisfied. In that case, they are of little value to the students they instruct since they are focused on survival. Isn't this the very premise of free lunch for students in school districts?

According to Maslow's hierarchy of needs, it's more difficult for anyone to self-actualize when they struggle to satisfy the most basic physiological needs for food, water, and shelter. In other words, safety, love and belonging, and esteem are complex dimensions that remain largely unsatisfied when the foundation of this pyramid is unstable. This struggle for existence in a poorly paying profession makes it more challenging to satisfy the role of an educator. Employee disengagement leads to low performance in our schools since teachers are overworked while working multiple jobs, making the case against zero a feasible alternative. So, I say, teachers first, then students. No teacher should feel compelled to work multiple jobs because their profession is unwilling to pay them a livable wage. The income gap between district administrators and teachers is of grave concern. Compensation is a significant source of contention that contributes to inadequate personal and professional satisfaction levels in life. The stress associated with diminished income is unnecessary from my perspective. As part of a solution to be heard, teachers should embrace the unions of their states and districts they serve in a show of solidarity to evoke the necessary compensation changes.

Content overload helps explain the case against zero grading practices with striking clarity. Advancements in technology and new content pose many challenges, especially when foundational content needs learning. Technology is evolving faster than we can master it. We are increasingly relying on technology more today than we did a decade ago. Technology is supposed to make our lives easier, yet many of us find ourselves consumed by it. This unhealthy consumption of technology makes the *case against zero* an attractive remedy for teachers and students. Although we are free, we find ourselves enslaved to technology. Being compelled to be available and constantly connected with people and our platforms contributes to an insufferable existence.

If stakeholders are concerned about graduation rates, why not reduce the material associated with the curriculum's scope and sequence? The material reduction is a better alternative to giving students grades they did not earn. The amount of information required based on the current content is so immense that keeping pace is challenging. This problem with too much content makes it difficult for students to acquire and master the material. Another viable option to this problem is to add a thirteenth grade to the traditional twelve. President Joe Biden similarly suggested that twelve years of education is no longer acceptable for students to compete in a global economy.[63] Even though emerging adulthood ends at age twenty-five, we still have twelve academic grades for primary and secondary education. As a result, people live five to six decades outside adolescence based on an average life expectancy of seventy-nine. In 1900, we lived on average until forty-seven and spent less time outside adolescence. Amusingly, we have far more information to learn today than we did twenty, thirty, and 122 years ago. Adding another grade level for high school would give teachers enough time to teach and students enough time to learn the material. This change in education could improve social competency and civic responsibility. This change in perspective could help youth build relevant competencies to compete in a global economy while improving the quality of their social lives. We could also consider eliminating the summer vacation. A two-week vacation after each academic quarter could give schoolteachers and students enough of a break to decompress from the rigors of education. A summer break is long and unnecessary for most people. These suggestions could be a prescription to the decaying educational system.

Developing students socially and intellectually is not enough unless we teach them moral and civic responsibility if the goal is to help them engage appropriately in a democratic society. The absence of such talents could lead to further anarchy and civil unrest that is far from peaceful. Social media and a poorly executed educational system are part of the problem that led to an unhealthy democratic engagement to discourse. Our country's democratic foundation appears cracked, and we need to repair it before it fractures. Acquiring knowledge is the

---

[63] Joe Biden, "President Joe Biden Delivers His First State of the Union Address," *CNBC*, April 28, 2021, https://www.youtube.com/watch?v=dggKaPXt0gI.

beginning. The goal is to use the knowledge through application for more profound meaning and understanding to enhance our Republic. Recently, advancements in technology led to disinformation and deep media fakes, which has caused people to question the fidelity of free speech. I am not here to debate this point. However, after six years of teaching high school, this is the first year that most of my students remain seated during the pledge of allegiance. As a result, those who stand with me are a minority. We listen to the pledge of allegiance while reflecting on our country's heritage. Although our country's union is imperfect, it is a living organism that continues to shine as a beacon of hope for the disenfranchised. This unpatriotic show of solidarity is becoming more popular among our youth. This phenomenon started with the age of disinformation and deep media fakes designed to spread fear among our populous with enormous success. We should all be gravely concerned since these students will come of age eventually. And when they do, they will change the geopolitical landscape in ways similar to Marxism. People should be mindful that we are one party away from socialism and one away from communism. Be warned about this theatre of absurdity before it's too late!

If I am right, we should expect lower degrees of grit and emotional intelligence because of the case against a zero-grading policy. People who lack the skills to cope with the demands of life would manifest more existential frustration that further disrupts societies and their lives as they become more nihilistic. A simple Google search (keywords: "the case against zero") will show this practice's systemic support, not moratorium.[64] Smithtown Central School District on Long Island supports the case against zero. They have a written policy that prevents teachers from entering any failing grades. However, is this policy specific, measurable, attainable, relevant, and time-based? If not, then it does not meet the minimum standard of SMART. This policy exists because it makes passing an academic quarter impossible

---

[64] "Teachers Defend 'No-Zero.'"

when grades are below 50 percent. Nevertheless, this district has a unique approach that implements this grading system fairly. Although there are good reasons for this policy, I find myself unconvinced of its effectiveness.

Academic practices should be measurable and grounded in scientific-based research. The Institute of Educational Sciences provides an online clearinghouse for educators with the most relevant research to guide their teaching practices.[65] All the elements associated with any scientific-based research need to be present to be an acceptable practice.[66] After close examination of this site, I cannot find any academic evidence to support the case against zero grading practices. We must ask if these policies teach students to be more resilient and grittier or provide them with more emotional knowledge to improve their overall intelligence. Are our life's challenges easier with half the effort? Does this practice nurture a fixed mindset or a growth mindset? A growth mindset would encourage flexibility, plasticity, and resiliency that is malleable rather than a fixed mindset that believes intelligence is biologically innate and unchanging. A rigid and inflexible condition is not desirable to the human condition, making for a boring life.

Life is not static; instead, it flows like a stream of water to the rhythm of life influenced by the changing currents that move us in new and unexpected directions. We must prepare ourselves for any eventualities as a captain redirects the sail on the deck of his ship in the direction of the wind to move the vessel forward. These changes require the flexibility to be resilient, perseverance and consistency to be gritty, and emotional knowledge to improve social interactions. These talents help us overcome some of life's inevitable challenges that make life feel impossible at times. Arming students with the proper skills to handle these challenges should enable them to create creative solutions

---

[65] Institute of Educational Sciences, https://ies.ed.gov/ncee/wwc/.
[66] Sharon A. Wynne, *Florida Educational Leadership Examination* (Melrose: XAMonline, 2018), 17.

tailored to our future. As a result of these talents, they should be able to maintain adequate levels of life satisfaction.

Policies written or unwritten, like the case against zero, can produce consequences that harm human ingenuity and achievement no matter how well-intentioned they might appear. I cannot understand the arguments in favor of such a philosophy since it produces a culture of mediocrity. Still, I recognize the pressures to accept it. This policy appears related to the business envelopes in teachers' mailboxes with names of failing students at the end of the quarter. Email would have been more efficient, but someone wanted this message to be anonymous and on paper. Teachers from other schools also received the same envelopes at the end of the quarter. Although we don't know who placed them there, the pressure to make sure a student passed was apparent. I don't blame any single person responsible for this decision, just as I can't blame a puppet's act when a puppet master controls the strings.

The motivation that drives this culture of mediocrity is partly rooted in the obsession with graduation rates. Perhaps a disinterested third party from an external source could audit the educational institutions nationally to uncover the short-term motivations that drive these practices. We might learn, for example, that grant funding demands specific outcomes at any cost. Losing sight of the big picture for the sake of graduation rates could create a lost generation scrambling to find their way in life.

Notably, I'm not referencing a lost generation like the literary writers and artists who emerged from the Great War. They produced some of the world's greatest literary works that inspired a generation of writers and painters from the Parisian culture. Writers, such as Sylvia Beach, T. S. Eliot, F. Scott Fitzgerald, Ernest Hemingway, James Joyce, Ezra Pound, Gertrude Stein, and Virginia Woolf, and artists, like Henri Matisse and Pablo Picasso, became household names. Although these artists exacted a criterion of artistic judgment from the external beauty that transcended contemporary rules of the masters, we should also note that they were mostly miserable. Their obsession for fame and immortality drove their behavior to extremes. At the same time, writers fleshed out more details from the outer world that redefined literary prose. Instead, I'm referencing concern that the case against zero will produce graduates who are unfit to embrace the demands of a complex society. As a result, they could appear lost for an entire generation as they struggle to develop the skills they never learned in secondary school.

I would have appreciated resistance to this grading approach when faced with my primary and secondary education challenges. The time is now for us to ask ourselves if we desire a culture of mediocrity or meritocracy. Once we answer this query, we can enact policies that benefit all stakeholders. We need a baroque application that reimagines education, not one that stifles it. Systemic changes to educational policy can shift the collective consciousness to a culture that rethinks standards that drive performance toward meritocracy. We can use innovative approaches that need to be grounded in a correct philosophy that is objectively measured and implemented to enhance the individuals and the communities.

College Years, Feelings of Inadequacy, and Changing Seasons

My first two years of college were the most difficult two years of my academic life. I was unable to meet specific proficiency levels for reading and writing. Even though I failed out several times, I would not give up. I kept going back and trying again, but—despite my best efforts—I could not pass the basic courses for reading, writing, and math. Although I excelled in mathematics earlier in primary education, teachers stopped challenging me in arithmetic because I lagged in all my other subjects. Their decision not to challenge me further exacerbated my secondary educational years. As a result, college mathematics had become an unforeseen (and unnecessary) problem.

Mathematics is considered a core science related to other subjects, such as social sciences, natural sciences, and biological sciences. However, teachers didn't explain how mathematics was relatable to the other core sciences during my primary and secondary education. This academic modicum of truth could have helped me master more complex subjects. We now call this approach "horizontal organization that describes a side-by-course arrangement where the content of one subject is made relative to the concepts of another related subject."[67] Earlier in my education, this approach would have helped me relate mathematics to other topics, such as economics, psychology, chemistry, biology, and physics.

Another issue thwarted my learning gains was how teachers assigned me to collaborate with other students. Homogenous grouping occurs when you group students with similar characteristics. This type of grouping design is practical. However, heterogeneous grouping is more effective. Students learn from their more cognitively advanced peers when assigned to cohorts who are different from them. Social cognitive theory helps explain how disadvantaged students learn by observing their classmates and imitating and duplicating their acts to nurture underdeveloped skills. My learning gains were retarded by the placement of unskilled instructors. Any learning gains to my intellect and emotional knowledge could have been more significant if I understood mathematics's importance to other subjects. This point is crucial because mathematics and behavior are two central maxims that help us understand the world. These two precepts help explain the microcosm for all living things and inanimate objects to the macrocosm of the whole universe that extends beyond humans and this tiny blue planet to the vastness of the cosmos.

Even after my early success in math, I developed an inferiority complex based on my formative years of education because of my poor performance. The work of Alfred Adler, a former follower of Freud,

---

[67] Wynne, *Highly Qualified Teachers*, 3.

helps shed light on the process by which such feelings of inadequacy can occur. Adler disagreed with Freud's insistence that sex and aggression were the driving forces underlying behavior. Instead, Adler asserted that "humans naturally strive to overcome inferiorities or deficiencies, both physical and psychological."[68] He further suggested that the process of striving for superiority can lead to an inferiority complex. Adler described people's "unhealthy need to dominate or upstage others as a way of compensating for feelings of deficiency."[69] Adler believed people unconsciously compensate to cover up their weakness of inferiority by striving for superiority. In addition, trying to upstage others constantly could lead to an unhealthy disengagement with people because of the desire to always feel superior across situations. I remember these feelings of inadequacy developing because I knew I was different, and other students recognized these differences. These early experiences left an indelible impression on my psyche. My mind was troubled. It left me with an uncomfortable perturbation that disturbed my interest in engaging with people. As a result, I retreated from human interaction. Still, I am not misanthropic because I enjoy many interactions with people as long as it is in short intervals.

During early childhood and adolescence, I felt similar to a deaf-mute. I felt this way. After all, I rarely tried because I had already given up on the idea of success at a young age. This discomfort caused me to retreat into the privacy of my thoughts. Turning inward to my interior felt the equivalent of being in a fortified citadel. This reclusive stronghold shielded me from any external assault from peers because it acted as my defensive shelter. It also offered me a prescription for the challenges and difficulties I faced. I would often comb my fingers gently through my hair while cogitating about life in this quiet space. At this time, I recognized the power of silence that would allow me to become an assiduous observer and an alert listener. For me, silence

---

[68] Quoted in Feist and Rosenberg, *Psychology*, 499.
[69] Quoted in Feist and Rosenberg, *Psychology*, 499.

transformed my perspective from feelings of loneliness to feelings of solitude.

The meaning of silence is of capital importance to me. It needs nurturing daily to germinate into the psyche. Once it takes root, it will transform the human condition. Yet as these examples illustrate, our culture constantly bombards us with superfluous sentiments that lead to unwanted noise that acts as an uninvited dictator in many of our minds. Consider this fact. Our brain is a dual-track mind that operates consciously and unconsciously. Processing information explicitly and implicitly is complex because we receive approximately 11 million bits of stimuli every second. Of this amount, we process fewer than fifty bits of stimuli consciously. The information processed is personally important to us, and some of it is essential for our survival. At the same time, most of it is unwanted noise. At first, I felt like a recluse because the silence amplified my inner thought, making me uncomfortable. Looking back, I realize that this was an instance important to my development of emotional intelligence. Rather than accepting and understanding only positive emotions, I embraced all of my emotional states. I attempted to acknowledge and adjust my negative emotions, even to the extent that I reframed a negative emotion such as loneliness to become an ambiguous positive feeling of solitude.

This paradigm shift from loneliness to solitude was essential to my cognitive and emotional development. Isolation feels more like an involuntary state, whereas solitude is a voluntary state of being. After this shift in perspective, I began to consider solitude a sanctuary, a quiet space where my thoughts could roam freely without fear of judgment and ridicule. This change in perspective also allowed me to become comfortable with my inner thoughts that were now more controlled. An occasional social faux pas, for example, could leave me feeling isolated from other people. As a result, I learned to button my lips to listen more and think before speaking. A lesson that I learned from the writings of St. Francis de Sales. To deal with any artificial interactions with people, I sequestered myself to the comforts of my imagination and my sacred place where such humiliations were unlikely. My thoughts kept me company. And I now believe that solitude and reflection are like trusted counselors that can help me navigate properly through life's various seasons.

Seasons are cyclical, and they bring different temperatures, making some climates feel pleasant, cool, cold, or warm. Each season brings new opportunities for growth or decay, as seen when spring ushers in the emergence of vegetation. Autumn appears when leaves fall from the branches of the majestic trees before winter reduces their former beauty to look like naked peasants. Life is also like this. Some seasons bring great abundance before the chaos, but order does return. The seasons now remind me of the business cycle, likened to a roller coaster. It follows a similar pattern that moves up and down and sideways, marking the ebbs and flows of life.

The market expansion represented a season of plenty that eventually peaked. Before peaking, there was a run-up of income and wealth. This season of growth strengthened my financial picture, and the hike to the summit appeared to be a promising reward. So fortunate that I couldn't ignore it, I felt empowered, wealthy, and happy. However, the spire of this cycle ends the expansion curve. At the peak of this cycle, the temporary vistas provided me with a moment of pride before the fall. Then came the slow descent over the precipice. This momentum gained traction as the gravity pulled downward to accelerate the fall. Before I knew what had happened, I was in an unwanted freefall as the violent contractions brought me crashing back to the earth's surface. The financial and professional success of the market expansion took years to achieve before the market contraction threw my life into a chaotic downward spiral almost overnight.

The season that brought me an abundance of milk and honey had now ended. It was easy to become emotionally attached to the things that enriched my life. Success doesn't occur overnight because the process requires years to nurture. Emotional attachment strengthens when we have more time invested in a person or anything else that pleases us. The more meaningful something is to us, the more difficult it is to let go. So it is no surprise that detaching myself emotionally from this season of life was tough. Divesting oneself emotionally from anything that brought enjoyment is not easy, but it is sometimes necessary. Like a garden, it was not always beautiful because much of the overgrowth needed pruning. To achieve a manicured garden, we sometimes need to prune and clear the branches to transform our image into something more radiant and refined.

Instead, for me, seasonal hardship or trauma acted like a fragmented memory trace that allowed me to recall some painfully lost memories. Years later, I remembered telling myself that great minds need less interaction with people during seasons of great scarcity. This thought brought me comfort because many extraordinary people have remarkable thoughts to keep them company. I was no different from these exceptional people. This epigram helped me feel better about myself. This single thought always calmed my mind in times of trouble or defeat. A passage from Ernest Hemingway's book *A Moveable Feast* captures this idea. He wrote, "The only thing that could spoil a day was people, and if you could keep from making engagements, each day had no limits. People were always the limiters of happiness except for the very few that were as good as spring itself."[70] This declarative sentence doesn't imply that I need no human interaction. Nevertheless, it suggests that too much interaction is unhealthy, and a silent space for reflection is required to be profitable.

Despite this type of interior solace, my inferiority complex followed me throughout my life. It is one reason for my depression that plagued me for many years. Although my inferiority complex produced some horrific effects on me, it was also the reason for my professional success. And yes, I often was driven to upstage other people to exert dominance while increasing my professional value. This constant need to prove myself created an uncomfortable tension under my skin. My mind

---

[70] Ernest Hemingway, *A Moveable Feast* (New York: Charles Scribner's Sons, 1964), 56.

constantly raced while my emotions were in a state of unwanted flux. This vibrating tension created an impulse that led to a thought for me to manifest later in my journey.

This internal pressure appears unhealthy, but it is like a piece of coal that undergoes a great deal of pressure from the earth's interior before transforming into a radiant diamond. As beautiful as the diamond is with some of its unseen blemishes to the naked eye, its birthmarks reveal the imperfections that it endured under extreme heat and pressure. New technologies can now change the color of a diamond in a laboratory for buyers interested in rare colors. Blue diamonds, for example, are rare and expensive to purchase. However, laboratories are now using an irradiated process to change clear diamonds to blue, which is more cost-effective and desirable. A cyclotron uses magnets to circulate the paths of protons and deuterons to transform the color properties from clear to blue. As coal transformed itself into a diamond, my personality went from dull to sparkling after being subjected to intense heat and pressure. Even now, my character became altered from the irradiation process, just like the diamond that changed colors into a unique blue that would become noticeable to many. This lengthy process helped prepare me for life's eventualities, and my unsettled mind transcended barriers like the fire that softens metal before the artisan shaped it into form.

Sometime around the age of twenty, I decided to go back to college as an adult learner. My decision to return to college was partly because some of my friends were graduating from college. At the same time, I worked as a machinist. However, a machine operator was economically undesirable. I referred to this season of life as my lost years. Working on lathes that curved and shaped metal into form was less exciting than working on sophisticated balancing machines. I preferred the latter. Yet the tedious repetition of balancing essential products for our nation's defense and aerospace program felt like a curse. I was at a crossroads, and I knew that I needed to decide if any paths in life were best for me.

This period was critical to my decision to return to a community college as a part-time learner while working as a machinist. During this time, I had to relearn how to study and master the art of being a good student. But of course, being a good student was a subjective value for me. Still, I made reasonable accommodation to my learning plan with no assistance. As part of this self-induced accommodation, I read every chapter assigned to me twice and sometimes three times. I also recorded lectures and listened to them at least twice, depending on the content's rigor, but always once. Eventually, I transferred from the community college to a university. The desire to understand other people and myself caused me to declare psychology as my major. Finally, I would graduate, and my commencement from the university proved that I was gritty and emotionally equipped to confront the morose of adversity.

Career Progress and Unforeseen Disaster

Throughout most of my career, I worked in personal and commercial banking. I excelled in banking and sales. The Bank of New York quickly promoted me from teller to platform to sales manager. These promotions were because of my communication skills and ability to grow assets and expand our brand within the financial center's footprint. Citigroup eventually recruited me as a business analyst. They conferred the assistant vice president title to me, which I held while managing a midsized business portfolio in New York. These titles were more impressive than my income. Yet my performance and ability to grow revenue in my assigned footprint proved impressive. Eventually, I left commercial banking for the more lucrative mortgage banking field.

I excelled as a mortgage originator in the call center for IndyMac Bank. My effort was recognized and rewarded by leadership. I remember working hard every day and most days were twelve hours long. I remember leaving the call center exhausted, but I always felt it was worth it because hard work yielded a high six-figure income. I felt like the top dog in my department, and I felt unstoppable. I remembered thinking, *Not bad for a guy with a learning disability.* The bank constantly rewarded me as a top performer with box seat tickets to watch the Angels and Dodgers play baseball at their respective stadiums. Trips to Vegas and specific events were another common benefit that we top performers enjoyed. I visited the Bellagio often and sometimes with all expenses paid. A penthouse stay was my favorite experience, especially when Beyonce and Jay-Z were in the adjoining suite. I felt deserving and entitled when the bank covered the visit because I knew how much revenue my production earned. My income, wealth, and stock options benefited from this season of enormous abundance. I thought this season of milk and honey had no end.

Then came the Great Recession. The recession felt unreal because it hit the financial markets suddenly, with force and power that felt like a powerful tsunami. You first notice the calm turquoise water recede from the shoreline as it makes its way out to sea. Although the water ebbed from the land, it created a calming deception. Then the sea levels rose skyward to a colossal height before assaulting the barren shoreline with a giant sea swell that ushered in a torrent of violent white water that crashed onto the shore. The unpredictable water made landfall while pushing inland quickly before taking its unprepared casualties and debris out to sea. I remembered listening to Warren Buffet's perspective on the crisis associated with the deterioration of the financial markets. He said something to the effect *that you never know who's swimming naked until the tide goes out.* In hindsight, this expression exemplifies how the banks acted like casinos that used their depositors' assets to finance the risk of mortgage banking and other speculative ventures. When the music stopped, so did the financial markets.

Although we recognized mortgage delinquencies had increased in the year leading up to the Great Recession, we thought it would be a mild correction. As my income continued to drop significantly, I remember thinking that the music was about to stop or at least change tunes. Hindsight bias clouded my judgment, as most people would like to believe they could see the financial collapse before it was a known catastrophe in the mainstream. I often told friends that I knew the Great Recession was coming. However, my indecision to change anything during this time suggests I was unaware of the impending financial crisis. I'd still have most of my wealth if I rebalanced my portfolio to a cash position. The stress in the financial markets was primarily related to the subprime market and the prime market's flex-pay mortgages. Many of these poor-quality loans were part of the mortgage-backed securities.

Companies, pension funds, and organizations big and small could not resist adding these speculative instruments to their investment portfolios. This decision added a tremendous amount of stress and risk to their balance sheets. As delinquency rates increased, regulators assessed the risk and exposure to many nonperforming assets as an economic threat to our economy. They realized that many of the mortgage assets that were now nonperforming were labeled investment-grade instead of poor credit quality or junk. Investors thought they were buying investment-grade securities, but their portfolios would be valued as junk and were now worthless.

The recession brought chaos and unwanted change to my life. My income dried up during this period, and my life now felt like an arid desert. Dry air swept across my barren landscape, devoid of any sustenance in this dry season that accompanied me like an unwanted rash. There was little solace or hope of any recompense from my profession now that the company imploded financially. During this period, I also watched my wages regress to levels not seen since I was a struggling college student. I was no longer the privileged top dog that people admired. Instead, I was economically vulnerable because my dominance waned as market conditions deteriorated. I was now the underdog, and the fight to climb the professional ladder again, one rung at a time, made me feel like a new hire: young and inexperienced.

During this period of my life, I lacked the enthusiasm necessary to maintain a positive attitude while engaging in this struggle to regain dominance. This shift from financial success to poverty was difficult for me to swallow. The pendulum of victory swung far to the one side of the success continuum. This success marked me with great abundance before the force pulled it violently back into poverty, where it would stay. I learned that unwanted change is uncomfortable and that environments are in a perpetual state of flux. Change tends to be unnoticeable to many people. Perhaps this is because its many dimensions make it more abstruse for many people to understand. Another possibility is that it is unnecessary to be consciously aware of much of the change around us unless it is a disruptive force. This destructive force causes the most unskilled observer to become aware of all of it.

Adaptability, Generativity, and Stagnation

Years ago, I read the book *Who Moved My Cheese?* To provide a basic summary of this work, Spencer Johnson wrote a bestseller based on how we deal with change in the workplace and our lives. This parable focuses on four mice and tells a story about how we deal with change based on our minds' complexity. The search for happiness under stressful conditions can make this journey feel like a daunting pursuit for some people yet a rewarding sojourn for those open to new experiences.

This famed fable intends that the reader can identify with one or more of the book's four central characters: Sniff and Scurry act like mice, while Hem and Haw are more like little people. Sniff and Scurry are simple-minded with good instincts. In contrast, Hem and Haw are like little people with complex brains. Like people, Hem and Haw have strong beliefs and emotions that can cloud their expectations while moving their behavior in a direction that ultimately proves to be less profitable. Although they all start their morning in the same way, by slipping into their jogging pants and sneakers, their experiences are profoundly different. At the same time, they run through the maze, searching for their cheese.

A summary of *Who Moved My Cheese?* follows:

The four imaginary characters depicted in this story—the mice, Sniff and Scurry, and the little people, Hem and Haw—are intended to represent the simple and the complex parts of ourselves, regardless of our age, gender, race, or nationality. Sometimes we may act like Sniff, who sniffs out change early, Scurry, who scurries into action, Hem, who denies and resists change as he fears it will lead to something worse, or Haw, who learns to adapt in time when he sees changing can lead to something better! Whatever parts of us we choose to use, we all share something in common: a need to find our way in the maze and succeed in changing times.[71]

This classic parable is essential for several reasons. First, Johnson makes a similar point to my earlier comments about a changing landscape. Resistance to change can be uncomfortable for some people because of the fear of something less rewarding. This type of person believes that the change is temporary and life will proceed as it once did. "Just be patient!" Second, some of us resist change only briefly before recognizing that we must adapt to the changing circumstances for something better. "I think something is wrong, and I will find something rewarding before it's too late!" Third, we recognize the trend associated with changing circumstances, and we embrace the change altogether and before others notice. "Let's innovate to stay ahead of the competition and avoid any losses related to inaction."

We realize that life ultimately represents change, and the quicker we adjust to change, the faster we can move on with our lives. Nevertheless, most people resist the process of change and ultimately prolong some of their negative experiences. This resistance could affect their overall well-being. With every loss or failure comes an unexpected

---

[71] Spencer Johnson, *Who Moved My Cheese?* (New York: G.P. Putnam's Sons, 1998), 16–17.

opportunity for growth. We should learn to accept defeat because it can allow us to see things from a different perspective. This internal struggle for equilibrium produces some of the greatest moments of productive change that one can experience due to psychic disturbances. Remember that failure is not a permanent condition that we should avoid but an opportunity to learn from it and move on with our life in the most productive way. Imagine how strange the world would appear if you decided not to get up after falling to the ground when you were an infant. Falling is a failure. Getting up is a successful outcome for this infant's ability to develop a growth mindset.

While giving a lecture at the college on Erik Erikson's psychosocial theory of development, a student asked me a provocative question about life satisfaction.[72] Generativity and stagnation are Erikson's seventh stage of development. This stage prompted the student to ask if regret was a universal feeling experienced when things in life turn out differently than expected. I liked her question since it showed that she was thinking about life's meaning. I said that regret was a universal feeling that helped us examine our actions to react to events differently in the future. People experience stagnation in middle age based on this stage. Perhaps they feel stagnation because they have not done enough to advance younger people's lives or maybe because they have been too focused on themselves.

Nevertheless, people interested in promoting youth are more likely to experience generativity during middle adulthood. And when they are in late adulthood, they are more likely to feel integrity for a life well lived, and they experienced despair if regret filled their thoughts. Therefore, people who lived with more generativity are more likely to have more integrity in late adulthood. They are also more likely to experience less regret, bitterness, and despair, which means they may achieve higher degrees of satisfaction in their lives.

There are qualitative differences between generativity and stagnation and between each of the stages of Erikson's theory. Each

---

[72] Satnrock, *Life-Span Development*, 22.

of these stages confronts the person with an existential crisis that needs resolution. The person might feel vulnerable during a problem as they seek and experience the cognitive conflict that consumes them. With mental conflict or loss comes an opportunity for intellectual and emotional growth. In this sense, my student's simple question about regret presented a quandary for me.

Rather than answering questions quickly, my teaching practice involves asking students for responses, which I did in this situation. A typical reaction from most of the students was that they had no regrets. Listening to their responses helped me remember the innocence of youth. It also helped me imagine what it would feel like to be young again. I remember thinking that their eyes were young and their experiences not yet ripe with maturity. Even now, I also knew that the passage of time would change how they understood regret. Perhaps people recognize that this question leaves them vulnerable. This question forces them to confront the ultimate truth that we all have regrets. Whatever their reasons, their responses might help insulate them from feelings of regret to avoid feelings of inferiority because they want to appear perfect and superior. After listening to their responses, they redirected the question back to me. I knew that I had to answer, but how should I answer without sounding too parochial?

While staring at the sea of people in front of me, I thought about how vulnerable I would like to be in the moment or whether I would be able to say something simple yet profound. I opted for the latter with a simple message while I thought about *Who Moved My Cheese?* After explaining the book's premise, I told students that my biggest regret in life was similar to Hem's. I said that much of my pain and suffering associated with the Great Recession could have been more palatable. My losses related to this event could have been more pleasant if I accepted my losses early on and moved on to the next best opportunity. It appears to me now that resisting change also prolonged my suffering, and I wish I could have been more like Sniff: an innovator. In the parable, Sniff is the one character whose simple-minded style enabled him to detect change. This ability to see differences meant that he could respond quickly to events to minimize losses in an unpredictable and changing world. A complex mind could overthink solutions to any problem rather than approaching it most simply. Sniff was more spartan in his approach to innovation than the complex mind of Hem that procrastinated change at the expense of a meaningful gain.

The change in my income and net worth embarrassed me. And I needed to make economies to my finances to cover basic needs. I was unemployed and later underemployed during this season of significant change. It made me feel unsatisfied and unproductive. Other colleagues experienced the same financial plight. To keep with the water metaphors from earlier, the market disruption in the financial markets was like a faucet from a cistern that flowed with predictability before the uncertainty turned it off. My home's equity was similar to this description of the cistern. Equity in my house was predictable and constant until adverse market conditions depressed home values that stripped away every dollar of equity. Foreclosures in my neighborhood were double-digit. They appeared to be worsening, so I kept adjusting the sale price downward until it sold. When I thought life could not become more complicated or uncomfortable, I was now homeless without a roof above my head or a bed to lie in. My savings ran out because of the expense of covering a mortgage and other unnecessary costs when I wasn't earning an income.

I didn't believe in a diversified portfolio of stocks at this moment in my life, so my entire stock portfolio was invested in IndyMac Bank. My decision to place all liquid assets into the company stock had been a mistake. The humorist Mark Twain said something to the effect of *putting all your eggs in one basket and watching it*. I guess you can say that I took this simple aphorism literally. So literally that I placed all my funds into IndyMac bank's common stock instead of adhering to the investment principles that advocated for a diversified portfolio to minimize risk. Building a more significant stock position in the bank was my objective to influence my next promotion and become a senior-level manager. Unfortunately, poor market conditions thwarted my plans. Instead, I found myself acting as the character Hem. I was shortsighted and unwilling to acknowledge changing market conditions. As a result, I lost the value of my entire stock portfolio when the bankrupted bank was placed into receivership by the Federal Deposit Insurance Corporation. At worst, I should have been like Haw, who decides to rebalance his portfolio to a cash position to preserve the value before losing it all. At best, I would have liked to be Sniff, the innovator. I could have bought put options that bet against the future health of IndyMac Bank before their troubled balance sheet went public. The apparent declining commission trend over two years should have signaled that something big was about to happen in the financial markets. Instead, I found myself asking, "Who moved my cheese?" I hunkered down in place and waited for the cheese to return. An innovator like Sniff would have gone back to university to earn an advanced degree during this period in anticipation of starting a new career in an unrelated field such as teaching. Still, at the time, I was behaving like Hem, not like the innovator Sniff.

When IndyMac bank went out of business, my shares were worthless, including all my stock options. Since my income and wealth evaporated as quickly as the morning dew, I found myself homeless. I slept in my Mercedes for some time. I learned that luxury vehicles might be comfortable to drive in, but they don't make comfortable beds. During this brief span, I also slept in my next employer's conference room before renting a modest room from friends. Capitalism felt like a cruel magic trick that could make income and wealth appear before reducing it and me to a pile of unwanted ashes.

The inferiority complex of my youth resurfaced. Feelings of inadequacy once repressed in my implicit memory reemerged to consciousness. And the unconscious memories brought back a treasure trove of painful memories that had faded in early adulthood. Regrettably, I misjudged the power of the unconscious mind to unlock repressed memories that felt abandoned. My financial success helped me leave these early childhood memories. In contrast, the Great Recession helped bring this dormant memory back into awareness as my income, equity, and wealth disappeared. When your district manager gives you money monthly for food and gas, you know life is hard. I do not say this to elicit any sympathy or pity because this story has a happy ending.

A colleague once described my ego as being as big as the Brandenburg Gate in Berlin. When I asked him why he compared my personality to the arch of peace, he politely said it was because of my brilliant mind and scintillating humor. He believed this was one reason for my financial success at the bank until the recession caused my personality to change. The charismatic charm that intoxicated people now felt as dry as a bottle of gin. Colleagues and clients have always admired my work ethic and resiliency for fighting through challenges. However, it appeared that my glowing star had faded from favor, and it still has. I didn't give my colleague's earlier comments about my ego being likened to the Brandenburg Gate much thought until I traveled on the grand tour of Europe.

The Brandenburg Gate marks the entry point to Berlin. It was built as a neoclassical monument by the Prussian king Frederick William II to glorify the country. The Quadriga is the goddess victory that stands tall and majestic. She commands a chariot being pulled by horses while watching over East Berlin and West Berlin from the top of this monument. The symbolism of this metaphor is important to me now because the gate survived World War II and the Cold War.

The Berlin Wall separated East Germany and West Germany, symbolizing division during the Cold War. While visiting Berlin, I stood at the west end of Unter den Linden Avenue while gazing intently at the Brandenburg Gate. I first thought about my relationship with the gate based on my former colleague's comments years earlier. I also thought about how different history would be if the Soviets removed the Quadriga from the top of this majestic gate. It appears peculiar that the Soviets didn't pull this important structure down since it represented hope for the unification of the German culture.

Another example worth noting is the famous speech delivered by former President Ronald Reagan in front of the Brandenburg Gate when he declared, "Mr. Gorbachev, tear down this wall." This speech marked the end of an era. However, the credit doesn't belong to Reagan exclusively. Historical negations typically ignore the powerful collaboration between Poland's Solidarity Movement and Pope John Paul II of the Roman Catholic Church that eventually influenced Reagan's political engagement to end communism with backdoor channels that culminated in a forceful speech. Thus, East Berliners and West Berliners could view this symbol of German strength and unity from both sides of the wall, which served as a powerful reminder that the fatherland would eventually liberate itself from foreign occupation before greatness returned.

Germany now has the fourth-largest economy since the iron curtain and the Berlin Wall collapsed. They are considered innovators in the fields of engineering and technology. Although my ego was battered and bruised like the Brandenburg Gate, I remembered thinking that the gate survived a world war and a cold war. Eventually, I would emerge from this season of chaos too. The Brandenburg Gate now represents peace and unity for the German people. Like the German people, my mind is now calm, peaceful, and unified.

I spent a great deal of time ruminating over the events surrounding my past. But unfortunately, calming my mind through idle conversation with friends proved to be an inadequate remedy. People tend to do one of several things during this type of conversation. They would first create an impression that they cared. However, this simple gesture was as hollow as a dead tree with no genuine effect. Their artificial talks led to uncaring solutions with a few facial gestures and outward pity expressions. After that, they urged me to get on with my life after saying that I would need to get a real job with honest wages. Their uncouth comments to me denoted jealousy for my success and pride for my fall. I now found their friendships insufferable since they were drunk with hatred. They were now an unwanted acquaintance with no opportunity for reconciliation even though I forgave them. Regrettably, many of these friends were less sensitive because they worked in nursing and teaching. In addition, these fields were more financially stable than mortgage banking during the Great Recession. Before leaving the talk, they would transition strategically to a faux topic midway through the conversation before departing. This form of structural confusion by friends who were tired of listening or caring caused me to think how insensitive and insufferable they were and how badly I wished to remove much of their income before telling them to get over it.

Another typical response was the constant complaining about the events that led to the market collapse and the continual reminder that life would take a while to return to normal. But of course, life never did return to normal. I am unsure why some people want to remember such an unpopular period in life. Even so, I recognize that people might not have the tools needed to get past it. People naturally defaulted to complaining about themselves, people, or life. I've listened to people complain my entire life. Complaining constantly to other people is taxing on the mind, and it's a source of irritation. It can drain any remaining life out of you. When we are without an emotional reserve to cope with this demand, the talks become more challenging. It appears that a hard life drains whatever reservoir remained in this type of situation. If you don't believe me, invite a person to have a conversation with you for thirty minutes longer than you want. Then watch how the meaningful tone changes in an unbecoming manner. They rarely offer a solution that advances your cause or provides solace. Then again, was there any viable solution that could have helped?

Recession and Personal Crisis

While market conditions worsened, conversations with friends gave me no solace. The discussions' solemn tone caused me to ask some difficult questions about my existence. I was officially in an existential crisis. This crisis has one of two outcomes, a nihilistic end or rebirth. I remember thinking that all roads led to Rome—and Freudian thought. In his book *Civilization and Its Discontents,* Freud wrote about the Roma Quadrata to explain that much of the ancient city remains hidden under centuries of earth's layers. Although we cannot see much of the hidden city, it doesn't mean that it doesn't exist, just as we are unaware of our unconscious thinking.

Our brain evolved from the oldest parts of the brain stem before the limbic system formed. These parts of the brain offer various functions that include unconscious thinking. Eventually the limbic system would evolve on top of the brain stem. This evolutionary development is essential to human survival. For example, the hypothalamus, part of the limbic system, regulates such basic drives as temperature, eating, drinking, and sexual desire. Compared to the hypothalamus, the hippocampus, a structure embedded deep in the brain's temporal region, is responsible for learning and memory. The hypothalamus and hippocampus are important structures that interact with the amygdala to help us understand emotional experiences. These implicit and explicit memories assist human survival. The last part of the brain's evolution is the outer layer of the cerebral cortex responsible for complex understanding and consciousness. It also suppresses the demands of basic drives when they are contrary to society's values. These were my thoughts as I walked the Via Sacra that connects the political and economic engine of the Roman Forum to Capitoline Hill. During this time, the death drive (as understood by Freud) surfaced in my thoughts; I could not love or find value in life. In his book *Beyond the Pleasure Principle,* Freud asserted that "we have made the antithesis between life and death instincts our point of departure."[73] He believed that the life and death phenomenon explains how eros flirts interactively with death. This creative interaction masquerades silently unseen in the background before the death drive manifests

---

[73] Sigmund Freud, *Beyond the Pleasure Principle,* trans. C. J. M. Hubback (London, Vienna: International Psycho-Analytical, 1922), 59, www.bartleby.com/276/.

in the foreground, acting as a powerful force that defines life and its end. Freud later remarked that "one might presume that the death drive operated silently inside the living being, working towards its dissolution, but this of course did not amount to a proof."[74]

Although the death drive didn't amount to any scientific proof, it doesn't necessarily mean that it is untrue. For example, we would never think that gravity doesn't exist even though "gravitation naturally does not exist for this observer," as Einstein wrote.[75] Think about this thought the next time you watch any object fall to the earth's surface. We should also think about the effects of gravity on young, impressionable minds. Infants, for instance, are like baby scientists. They play with their food before eating it. Infants can test the effects of gravity and the support of the floor when they are sitting in their high chairs. We should consider their experiment the next time we see an infant throw mashed potatoes onto the floor. Some parents will get upset since they want the infant to eat their food, not play with it. Parents will typically squawk in anger at the infant who messes their clean floor or muddies their face. I say, "Let them be a curious scientist that explores the peculiar effects of gravity. Once their thought experiment is satisfied, they will begin to wear their food less and eat it after about eight months of age."

The consequences associated with stifling an infant's curiosity could have profound effects for them later in adolescence. Infants could learn mistrust instead of learning to trust adults during infancy if their curiosity and behavior become inhibited. Suppose adults suppress and punish an infant's curious nature. In that case, they are more likely to experience shame and doubt instead of autonomy during early adolescence.[76] These issues of mistrust, trust, doubt, and autonomy are part of the eight psychosocial stages of development addressed by Erikson, mentioned earlier in this chapter. This teaching of mistrust

---

[74] Freud, *Civilization and Its Discontents*, 63.
[75] Albert Einstein, *Relativity: The Special and General Theory* (New York: Holt, 1921), 77.
[76] Santrock, *Life-span Development*, 18th ed., 22.

could lead to decreased curiosity, limiting the child from seeking new opportunities. Eventually, the child would learn to become more reactive to events rather than setting out to solve a problem. Although infantile amnesia prevents me from remembering this occurrence, my parents gave me this understanding. They often squawked at me for similar reasons before modifying their parenting style toward me in early adolescence. In short, solving problems is more gratifying than being reactive.

I'll return to my existential crisis. Freud said that the "more fruitful idea was that a portion of the drive was directed against the external world and then appeared as a drive that aimed at aggression and destruction."[77] During my economic crisis, I kept thinking how difficult it would be to exist for another six months. Unless I could transform my mind and convert this pile of muck into a precious stone, I would find life's existence meaningless and difficult to continue this journey. Similarly, eros was finally ready for the death drive to manifest toward the end of Freud's life. Sensing his end was near, Freud's friend administered a heavy dose of morphine that caused him to lapse into a coma before dying. Freud's long-held view that the death drive would eventually overpower eros thus manifested.

Frankl's *will to meaning* was likewise absent from my psyche. Lacking the will to find meaning in the chaos of my life was a dangerous place for me. My thoughts felt like a plague of some sort that could affect all the constitutional parts of my body. I wanted my end to occur, but how? Old age is years away from me. I had reached an extremely dark place—an abyss that drove me to self-destructive behavior—and didn't care. The etiology of suffering that contributes to lower degrees of life satisfaction can be considered a plague of some sort. Albert Camus described a physical epidemic that swept across the French Algerian city of Oran in his book *The Plague*.[78] He draws a comparison between the biological and physical plague that brings about a quick death and

---

[77] Freud, *Civilization and Its Discontents*, 63.
[78] Albert Camus, *The Plague* (New York: Vintage, 1991, first published 1947 by Gallimard).

a plague of the mind that renders a person incapacitated. Likewise, thinking disorders can plague a person with recurring thoughts that become obsessive, and acting on these thoughts can lead to compulsive actions that bring about superfluous and undesirable behavior.

Frankl's work on logotherapy has particular importance to me for some reasons. First, it helped explain how pain, guilt, and death would limit human existence. Second, his new therapy developed due to his involuntary stay at the Auschwitz and Dachau death camps that resulted from the nationalistic pride of the Nazis that led to a vanguard of crime. Some years ago, I thought about Frankl's involuntary stay at the Dachau camp because of my visits. My first curious observation was the disfigured rails for the trains that transported prisoners from various parts of Europe's Jewish quarters and other camps when approaching the entrance. To the right of the rails stood a damaged platform crumbling from the passage of time. However, it still serves as a powerful reminder of the human atrocities directed at Jewish people at this death camp. This platform marked the end of the line for the holocaust train. At the same time, it also marked the beginning of dissatisfaction for many involuntary guests.

The Jewish and political detainees walked a short distance from the platform toward the main iron-barred gate. The insidious slogan "Arbeit Macht Frei" was written on the gate. This sinister motto is translated from German to English as "Work Sets You Free." I remember thinking that Frankl walked through this gate after exiting the train. He must have read this epigram that appeared humorous to the Schutzstaffel but satirical to the Jewish captives. I wondered if Frankl was influenced by this catchphrase on the gate when he first talked about "unemployment neurosis,"[79] a type of depression he diagnosed in young patients.

Further, Frankl noted, "Being jobless was equated with being useless, and being useless was equated with having a meaningless

---

[79] Frankl, *Man's Search for Meaning*, 135.

life."[80] This quote from Frankl's book was particularly meaningful to me during this period of my life. I understood this reality about unemployment and underemployment, which left me identifying with Frankl's existential analysis about the relationship between work and life's meaning. I knew that unemployment neurosis would make me feel unproductive, and it would probably worsen my misery. This phenomenon inflicted many people, and "as soon as they could fill their abundant free time with some sort of unpaid but meaningful activity—their depression disappeared although their economic situation had not changed and their hunger was the same."[81]

Although horrifying, the epigram pointed to a central truth. People should work while staying at the encampment to feel helpful to those in the camp, not because they hoped to be freed but by working and caring for their comrades. Thus, Frankl found *a will to meaning* by helping other people while at the death camp. Frankl also addresses the case for tragic optimism in *Man's Search for Meaning*.

> In the concentration camps, this behavior was paralleled by those who one morning, at five, refused to get up and go to work and instead stayed in the hut, on the straw wet with urine and feces. Nothing—neither warnings nor threats—could induce them to change their minds ... they took out a cigarette from deep down in a pocket where they had hidden it and started smoking. At that moment we knew that for the next forty-eight hours or so we would watch them dying. Meaning orientation had subsided, and consequently the seeking of immediate pleasure had taken over.[82]

This tragic optimism is a phenomenon present in our industrial

---

[80] Frankl, *Man's Search for Meaning*, 135.
[81] Frankl, *Man's Search for Meaning*, 135.
[82] Frankl, *Man's Search for Meaning*, 134.

societies as we struggle to find meaning in life. At the same time, we grope through the darkness in vain. Frankl says, "A human being is not one in pursuit of happiness but in search of a reason to become happy."[83] If we can will our meaning into existence, we could transform our suffering into much more than any accomplishment or achievement that transcends our reality. In this sense, a rule to strive for could be converting guilt to something more meaningful for an improved presence and always taking responsibility for your actions before it's too late.

Once I grappled with the Great Recession circumstances, I decided to go back to university for an advanced degree. The change in my employment would prove to be an unwanted but necessary event that led me back to university, searching for a more rewarding career. After completing my graduate degree in psychology, I secured a position as a teacher while working on a doctorate in psychology. The doctoral process had a profound effect on me. It changes the doctoral candidate in a way that no one can understand unless you go through the brutal hazing. After many iterations and few submissions, the journey ended with presenting my manuscript to a panel. My faculty mentor and chair as well as committee members said, "Congratulations, Dr. Ott. Welcome to the academy of scholars." When the zoom call ended, I felt my body decompress from the stress after the hundreds of hours of work that culminated at this moment, and my sober emotion felt stoic. A life's work of experiences has culminated in this moment of extreme gratitude.

However, even after this tremendous achievement, I experienced difficulty related to the university's prestige I attended. Therefore, my education remains a source of regret and dissatisfaction. As an undergraduate, I graduated from a "Research 1 (R1)" institution; my graduate and doctoral degrees were not from such an institution. Our culture continuously ranks intelligence according to the colleges or

---

[83] Frankl, *Man's Search for Meaning*, 133.

universities you attend. In other words, the better the university, the better the faculty. I remember applying for a full-time position at Indian River State College. A colleague of mine bluntly said that I needed to hope that a candidate doesn't apply for this full-time faculty position from an R1 university. That way, I could be a serious candidate. She said I stood a better chance of being hired if my advanced degrees were from Stonybrook University like my undergraduate degree was, but they weren't. Educational bias directed at people from less prestigious universities is subtle discrimination. It harms people economically and professionally. When they qualify for the post, it's as bad as not offering a position to someone based on their race, ethnicity, or religious practices. To say that educational bias doesn't exist is like saying that implicit bias is a bunch of malarkey. Think about your internal thoughts and nonspoken reaction to anyone that tells you they did not graduate from an R1 or R2 university.

Academic snobbery is a natural phenomenon because people always want to feel that their credentials are more valuable than others. People adhere to ranking as a source of achievement. I never wanted any advanced degrees until a disruption in the financial sector changed my path in life. Going back to university was not easy as an adult learner. It is not easy to attend an R1 institution as an adult with financial commitments and obligations that make entering university more difficult later in life. For these reasons, I attended online universities. Prestigious universities improve your employment prospects and earning potential. Graduating from Georgetown, Harvard, Stanford, the University of Southern California, and Yale makes a difference to a student's future career. However, it doesn't mean that their graduates are more skilled than the less reputable universities. If a student doesn't get into the best schools, they become sad or depressed. They even feel defeated. Although I am not depressed, it saddens me to think that my advanced degrees don't hold as much value. At least in the eyes of some academic colleagues and members of the public as my undergraduate degree.

When we think about the word *prestigious*, we think of a highly reputable university or award. Other synonyms associated with prestige include an attitude of elitism, honor, respect, and reputation. However, the word has its origin in the sixteenth century as being related to the practice of conjuring tricks, illusions, or deception. According to *The Oxford English Dictionary*, the most frequently used definition of *prestige* is "influence or reputation derived from achievements, associations, or character, or (esp.) from past success; a person's standing in the estimation of others."[84] However, the history of the word is more related to deception. The etymology of *prestigious* is rooted in the middle French language to mean "an illusion; a conjuring trick; a deception, an imposture"[85] and was used as early as 1372 to represent an illusion produced by magic.

Many prestigious universities got caught up in the Federal Bureau of Investigation's criminal case known as Operation Varsity Blues.[86] The admissions scandal captivated the nation. It caused many people to raise an eyebrow at the deceptive admissions practices designed to perpetuate the system of elitism that is now falling from favor, though not fast enough. I can't help but think about how qualified people have often been overlooked for high-paying positions because they did not graduate from the most prestigious universities. Many graduates were admitted under pretenses and graduated after speaking to or paying the right person. This thought consumes me and produces a great deal of dissatisfaction, primarily when I think about qualified candidates passed over for interview consideration. I can personally relate to these feelings of inadequacy. They make me feel like a pseudoscientist. Therefore, read and absorb as much knowledge as possible, and don't

---

[84] *Oxford English Dictionary Online*, 3rd ed. (2021), s.v. "Prestige," https://www-oed-com.colorado.idm.oclc.org/view/Entry/150864?redirectedFrom=prestige#eid.
[85] *OED Online*, "Prestige."
[86] John Anderson, "'Operation Varsity Blues: The College Admissions Scandal' Review: Dishonor System." *Wall Street Journal*, March 16, 2021, https://www.wsj.com/articles/operation-varsity-blues-the-college-admissions-scandal-review-dishonor-system-11615930560.

be concerned about the prestige associated with universities. Strive not only for achievement or accomplishment that lasts a short time but also direct your energy to the community's affairs, the development of people, and toward a satisfying life. People will learn that you are skilled and highly qualified eventually. Nevertheless, we need to work smart and work on all facets of our personalities before people offer us the recognition we seek.

A few more examples are needed to support the illusions and trickery associated with the word *prestige*. We spoke briefly about the institutional prestige of education. Now we turn to Machiavellian economics and the institutional dishonesty that failed to operate from a philosophy of ethics. Economics is essential to an economy. When people run these businesses of economic influence with wrongdoing, then economic instability disrupts the social fabric of our lives. We become sad, depressed, miserable, paralyzed with fear while emotionally despondent to people, and dissatisfied with the quality of life when severe economic instability disrupts our lives. Since the Great Recession is the source of much of the pain and suffering that I endured, it appears fitting to discuss the economic behavior in more detail. First to be addressed is some work from moral philosophers and economists. Then I will discuss the institutional dishonesty of some investment houses, but not all of them since there are too many examples for this book. The goal is to present helpful information in this section written in an economic vernacular that is culturally relevant for people to understand.

The father of capitalism and a moral philosopher, Adam Smith, wrote about economics. He mentioned the "invisible hand" once in his book *The Wealth of Nations*.[87] Perhaps he wanted this term to appear as invisible as possible from the astute observer because unseen forces drive a free market economy. The attentive observer cannot detect these unseen forces as free markets function most efficiently

---

[87] Adam Smith, *The Wealth of Nations* (Oxford, England: Bibliomania.com Ltd, 2002), lccn.loc.gov/2002564559.

when self-interested traders operate silently in the background. They negotiate the terms of something to buy from someone wanting to sell them something of value. If the transaction terms are agreeable, then the transactions close between those involved. The price of bread, for example, is of no concern if two people negotiate a reasonable price, even if the price appears outrageous to others. However, the insertion of outside forces makes a fair negotiation for bread cost between buyers and sellers a less desirable outcome. This external influence could artificially drive the price of bread up or down, making the transaction less attractive to those wanting it. For example, suppose an external force artificially creates a shortage of the baker's yeast to make bread. In that case, the market responds with higher prices, and if the baker's yeast artificially floods the market, then the cost of bread falls. This market manipulation is not advantageous to the buyer or seller of bread. Instead, it is to the market manipulators who tried to profit by shorting a product or artificially pumping up its price above support levels.

In the same way, this perception of deceit created the panic needed for movement in the stock or commodity for a minority of operators to profit. Thus, external influences are essential when understanding how prices become irrational. When external forces are absent, the intended consequence of the invisible hand influences traders freely to purchase and sell goods and services at reasonable prices based on self-interest. Therefore, the invisible hand brings equilibrium to a competitive market that controls the consumer demands' supply of goods and services. Smith believed the invisible hand influenced free trade best when laissez-faire economics allowed capital markets to function without interference. Unfortunately, government policy interferes with laissez-faire economics, so people cannot buy and sell freely.

We should not forget about the prestigious investment houses of Wall Street that shut down at the beginning or during the Great Recession. Wall Street operators are the new warlords. Although they don't battle in the traditional sense, they are master chess players who strategically fight competitors in the market, intending to run them out of business. Their risk is a gambit that sacrifices any unimportant pawn as a calculated risk for market advantage. Often, their risk is insatiable because the desire to win big at any cost overrides their ability to reason.

We should expect an economic disruption in the future when the pawns learn to think for themselves. At the same time, they will eventually coordinate a workable strategy that changes the economic landscape because Wall Street operators consciously ignored the warnings of their consumers. The Occupy Wall Street movement is an example of how the pawns coordinated an open protest against many firms that hustled the economic system that caused the Great Recession. Movements like Occupy Wall Street could precursor the next significant economic disruption. So it is wise for capitalists to bear this point in mind. For example, technology now exists for social movements to coordinate strategic deposit runs on banks. This actionable risk by disruptive agents could inflict havoc on our financial institutions and people's social life. After all, the world would appear much different if the king of France, Louis XVI, listened to the peasants' and the aristocrats' complaints before the French revolution. Although he was born of high birth, he proved an unsuitable leader for quelling the insurrection of the people's revolution. When the people of Paris questioned the King's absolute authority, they gathered on the cobblestone street fronting Le Procope before marching to the palace of Versailles. Instead, Paris became a theatre of revolution, providing Europe with a model for society's political and social realignment that continues to reverberate today. As observed with Robespierre, we should know that people eventually turn on their masters. He was a leader in the revolution before suffering the same fate as the monarchy that he aimed to end. Instead, Paris witnessed three revolutions stretching across two empires in less than a century. The collapse of the monarchy paved the way for Marxist ideology fifty-nine years later. As a result, we are still grappling with Marxist influence in American society and the global geopolitical landscape that plagues our academic and financial institutions in opposing means.

Before presenting some examples, I want to discuss some of the books that influenced this section. Professor Emeritus John Kenneth Galbraith from Harvard's economics department wrote about the events that led to the Great Depression in his book *The Great Crash, 1929*.[88] The book focused on the human behavior of the Roaring Twenties that influenced the speculative bubble of investments that caused the stock market to collapse. Insiders usually downplay the influence of Wall Street, but Galbraith suspected that their role was far more involved than believed. In particular, the Florida property bubble during the Roaring Twenties caused many commodities and common stocks to soar to new heights. Many investors from the middle classes were becoming rich from the speculative land deals that influenced the irrational prices before crashing. These are some of the events that led to Black Thursday, and the stock market crash parallels the Great Recession. Galbraith noted in a documentary that we should expect another market disruption soon. He believed that people have short-term financial memories and the economic temptation to get rich makes them irrational.

Inflicting harm to any economy is not a new phenomenon. During the Dutch Golden Age, the speculative bubble related to tulips became the fourth leading export in the seventeenth century.[89] Investor speculation in tulip futures became a hot commodity, even for investors who had never seen them. Tulipmania caused many irrational investors to speculate about the commodity price. As a result, tulips became more expensive than a carriage and several horses and a half a ton of cheese. The ridiculous costs of tulips drove the market price to unprecedented levels that had no more support, and the Dutch stock market crashed. Many foolish investors went from riches to poverty once the music stopped playing.

---

[88] John Kenneth Galbraith, *The Great Crash, 1929* (Boston: Houghton Mifflin, 1955).
[89] Galbraith, *The Great Crash*.

Insiders wield more control than previously believed on Wall Street. Galbraith noted a similar point in his book *The Economics of Innocent Fraud: Truth for Our Time*. He explained how avarice led to scandal in the ivory suites of some reputable corporations that damaged the economy and people's social lives.[90] Furthermore, he observed how federal penalties were smaller than the profit earned from corporate greed. In other words, Galbraith believed that corporate fraud occurs more frequently because it makes sense when the gains exceed the cost of the fines. This unscrupulous corporate behavior means that market instability is more likely to occur. How different would corporate behavior be if the financial penalties were twice the amount of the actual fraud? Galbraith viewed market disruptions as harmful to society because economic inequality, unbalanced production, and price instability were averse to societal needs.

Galbraith's book *The Good Society: The Humane Agenda* was a noble attempt to examine the foundation of our economy through a societal lens before making suggestions on creating a better culture for all people.[91] Although his views appear on the left side of the political spectrum as a socialist, he is more moderate than one might expect. He focused on people from various social classes with an economic plan to provide more economic opportunities for all stakeholders to have a more enjoyable social life. His humane agenda is a rational social contract and financial plan that makes sense for society, not a few elitists aimed at exclusive wealth acquisition.

Galbraith's genius rests on his ability to view economics and political structures through a historical lens. His critique is an honest attempt to understand and address what we do right and the destructive political and economic forces that disrupt businesses and market cycles. Steep periods of growth bring violent contractions that further

---

[90] John K. Galbraith, *The Economics of Innocent Fraud: Truth for Our Time* (Boston: Houghton Mifflin, 2004).
[91] John K. Galbraith, *The Good Society: The Humane Agenda* (Boston: Houghton Mifflin, 1996).

lead to falling gross domestic products, lower household incomes, and higher levels of unemployment and underemployment. In short, all stakeholders in the economy lose when capital investments become uncertain and unstable. The desire for prestige drives human behavior toward acquiring wealth at any cost, including the drive to improve economic perceptions that influence power and legislation. A good society will never be a perfect utopia because of human involvement.

Nevertheless, it is pragmatic to enhance people's lives with a sustainable approach to meeting the demands of the humane agenda. Suppose we could let go of our ego and desire for wealth and fame. In that case, we would be more equipped to nurture a collective consciousness that could change how society approaches economics and education for a better social life. We learn to be selfish, but our innate archetype is social and cooperative. We manifest evidence of aggressive tendencies when threats appear. When systems imbalances occur between society and these archetypes, chaos ensues.

A social contract for a good society is not hostile to capitalistic structures. It doesn't mean that a good society should empty its financial coffers for unproductive people either. We are a meritocratic society that should reward ingenuity and innovation in technology and education to improve our lives while learning to be better people. This type of society based on merit means that we need to create an environment that gives everyone an equal chance to become unequal. As a result, giving people the tools they need to succeed should strengthen our democratic process for a more equitable society. Excluding a portion of the population from economic participation means less ingenuity and productivity and less progress. Not having gone to one of the right prestigious universities should not bar a candidate from entry to economic opportunity. Market disruptions disrupt the lives of people, corporations, governments, and universities. The economic effects during such market downturns could cause significant mental and physical troubles among people and make their situation difficult, as it did for me. The impact of severe market turmoil could last an entire decade.

When we think about wisdom, we think about older people. This reality is because wisdom emerges decades after our youth. After all, it takes a lifetime to understand our collective experiences. In other words, wisdom is a virtue that takes time to nurture. People's experiences change throughout life, and the folly of our youth begins to reshape with insights that emerge in the afternoon of our life in the form of wisdom. These changes bring new insights based on what worked in the past and what is currently not working. The ability to make changes brings life's actions into harmony with nature's wisdom. When conscience betrays the virtues we aimed to develop in our lives, then a thinking disorder ensues. Machiavellian economics could be considered a thinking disorder that shapes institutional culture. Institutional haughtiness led to stinginess, avarice, and selfishness. Suppose we plumb the recesses of our minds. In that case, we might learn that the repetitive nature of thinking about making more money with unbridled creative energy might fashion methods that could be ethically concerning. Employing these thoughts into action is the compulsion that acts on the obsessive thoughts that enhance our economic position. Although not all wisdom is a trait bestowed on many seasoned managers, they do command the financial resources at some distinguished companies that make them dangerous to people's social lives.

Lehman Brothers is an excellent example of disaster capitalism because it was one of Wall Street's wealthiest firms.[92] It was so successful that graduates from some of the most prestigious universities worked in leadership positions for Lehman Brothers.[93] It was an old

---

[92] James Mackintosh, "Lehman's Lessons, 10 Years Later," *Wall Street Journal*, September 6, 2018, https://www.wsj.com/articles/lehmans-lessons-10-years-later-1536255748; Corrie Driebusch, "Lehman's Last Hires Look Back," *Wall Street Journal*, September 7, 2018, https://www.wsj.com/articles/lehmans-last-hires-look-back-1536321600.

[93] Jeff Guo, "The Jobs That Really Smart People Avoid," *Washington Post*, January 12, 2017, https://www.washingtonpost.com/news/wonk/wp/2017/01/12/the-jobs-that-really-smart-people-avoid/.

institution where wealth and prestige were centralized. Poor and questionable accounting practices and securities fraud were reasons listed for Lehman Brothers' failure. Although this firm survived the Civil War, two world wars, and the Great Depression, it could not survive the Great Recession.

Another example of disaster capitalism is Bear Sterns. They emerged in the early part of the Roaring Twenties. They were one of the darlings of Wall Street and created large six- and seven-digit incomes for employees with unspeakable wealth. Bear Sterns went from healthy to insolvency within three days after investors withdrew capital and lenders pulled back access to warehouse lines of credit. When executives realized that their cash position was in jeopardy, they rang the alarm bells to attract a capital infusion.[94] Disaster capitalism found its way into the institutional walls of this prestigious institution destined for financial ruin before the fire sale of their company caught the attention of a suitable buyer, J. P. Morgan.[95]

Although Bear Sterns survived the Great Depression and World War II, it could not survive the storm of the Great Recession. Experts and analysts cited a few reasons for their collapse. First, the firm took a bullish position on the stock market, which carried inherent risk to its balance sheet. They were bullish on creating two mortgage-backed securities hedge funds that credit-rating firms rated as investment-grade.[96] Standard & Poor rating services, Moody's investor's services, and Fitch ratings were sued by the liquidators of Bear Sterns, citing inaccuracy in their inability to rate these assets properly.[97] A class-

---

[94] Kate Kelly and Serena Ng, "Bear Stearns Bails Out Fund with Big Loan," *Wall Street Journal*, June 23, 2007, https://www.wsj.com/articles/SB118252387194844899.
[95] Robin Sidel, Dennis K. Berman, and Kate Kelly, "J.P. Morgan Buys Bear in Fire Sale, as Fed Widens Credit to Avert Crisis," *Wall Street Journal*, March 17, 2008, https://www.wsj.com/articles/SB120569598608739825.
[96] Kelly and Ng.
[97] Jeannette Neumann, "Bear Stearns Fund Liquidators Sue Credit-Rating Firms," *Wall Street Journal*, July 10, 2013, https://www.wsj.com/articles/SB10001424127887323740804578597883074252160.

action lawsuit finally brought a settlement that J. P. Morgan agreed to pay. Consistent with Galbraith's insight about innocent fraud—as mentioned previously in this chapter—the payment for the class-action compensation was less than the revenue generated for the mortgage-backed securities. J. P. Morgan paid a bargain price of $500 million to settle the mortgage-backed securities valued at nearly $18 billion.[98]

These bullish strategies on mortgage-backed securities were complex structures for the refinancing of mortgage-backed securities. Pooling these assets to sell to institutional investors was common practice. This practice is not necessarily unethical or harmful if the investors know what they are buying. Credit-rating agencies rated these structured funds at Bear Sterns as having good credit quality. However, these structured funds were sold to investors as high-grade investment products even though many of the packaged securities were low investment-grade or junk. Why would they manipulate the ratings on these products? The answer is one of institutional collusion and public trickery from these prestigious firms. High investment grade ratings meant they didn't have to pay high-interest payments on these debts. A favorable rating indicated that the assets were of good quality and should continue to perform. If, however, credit-rating agencies rated these instruments correctly, investors would have known that both risk and reward were greater, despite the likelihood of the asset not performing. I believe this was the motivation behind Bear Sterns' securitization model that led to conspiring with the credit-rating firms. Interestingly, many of the employees who had graduated from prestigious universities made these deceptive decisions of trickery. When these assets stopped performing and credit defaults mounted, cash flow dropped to dangerous levels and they sold the firm's holdings at reduced value instead of filing bankruptcy.

The last example of prestige to present is Merrill Lynch, founded five

---

[98] Julie Steinberg, "J.P. Morgan to Pay $500 Million to Settle Lawsuit," *Wall Street Journal*, January 9, 2015, https://www.wsj.com/articles/j-p-morgan-to-pay-500-million-to-settle-lawsuit-1420836735.

months before the Great War. Like Lehman Brothers and Bear Sterns, some of our nation's "brightest," from the best universities, worked at Merrill Lynch. They were a significant player in the subprime mortgage market. Unfortunately, their balance sheet had too many mortgage-backed securities and unhedged collateralized debt obligations. As a result, when the revenue for the investment firm declined, they weren't able to manage the debt. Merrill Lynch was now on the verge of insolvency when the United States Secretary of the Treasury, Henry Paulson, intervened and brokered a deal between Merrill Lynch and Bank of America.[99] Although they didn't go out of business, their troubled balance sheet became Bank of America's property and the source of many of the institution's financial concerns. The Great Recession could have been easier to contain and control if the financial institutions fell like a line of dominos, but they didn't. Instead, each financial institution was like a popcorn kernel that heated up before popping randomly with great intensity. The unpredictable nature of each kernel popping randomly led to tremendous economic uncertainty. This instability created stress in the financial sector and unwanted pressure for the Treasury.

Belief in the free markets is, of course, central to capitalism. Yet their bullish bets in risky areas with market manipulation poked the bear, ushering in an era of adverse consequences. These results were increased student loan debt, a weakened job outlook, lower fertility rates, and a gloomy and pessimistic future. When investment houses used manipulation tactics, the assets traded on the stock market and credit defaults increased, which inflicted harm to shareholders and all stakeholders of the economy. These outcomes influenced many other people, including me, to feel isolated, lost, and largely unsatisfied with life. Capitalists often scream with great conviction against socialism. Still, they asked for social assistance when a capital infusion was beneficial. Without a financial injection, their way of life becomes an existential threat. To avoid

---

[99] Matthew Karnitschnig, Carrick Mollenkamp, and Dan Fitzpatrick, "Bank of America to Buy Merrill," *Wall Street Journal*, September 15, 2008, https://www.wsj.com/articles/SB122142278543033525.

dissolution, banks and investment houses lobbied Paulson at the Treasury for the Troubled Asset Relief Program (TARP). This program emerged after the collapse of Lehman Brothers, Bear Sterns, Countrywide, and IndyMac Bank.[100] Corporate nepotism could have influenced Paulson's decision regarding which firms would survive and which would fail. After all, Henry Paulson was an alumnus of the prestigious Harvard University and former chairman and CEO of Goldman Sachs before occupying the office of the United States Treasury.

The Glass-Steagall Act of 1933 emerged in the aftermath of the Great Depression. This legislation placed a barrier between banks and investment houses. The repeal of the Glass-Steagall Act in 1999 meant that commercial banks and investment houses could operate as one.[101] Banks and investment firms could now remove the barrier separating banks from investment houses. Repealing the Glass-Steagall Act gave investment firms the tools they needed to expand their influence on the market to acquire more wealth before the Great Recession.

A concerning trend emerged in the aftermath of the Great Recession. More specifically, a 2011 statistic reported an alarming truth about the concentration of wealth.[102] The wealthiest 20 percent controlled 84 percent of the wealth. To say this another way, 80 percent of people are fighting for 16 percent of the wealth. This economic tension we feel collectively is why we work multiple jobs simultaneously because 16 percent of the remaining wealth is not enough to satisfy the daily needs of 80 percent of the population.

Although two centuries have passed since the French Revolution, *A Tale of Two Cities* remains culturally relevant today. It provides a literary example of this idea. This epoch novel captured the people's

---

[100] Alan Zibel and Jeffrey Sparshott, "TARP Watchdog: Big Banks Got Unfair Advantage," *Wall Street Journal*, March 17, 2011, https://www.wsj.com/articles/SB10001424052748703818204576206482220073322.

[101] John Carney, "The Secret History of Glass-Steagall," *Wall Street Journal*, July 19, 2016, https://www.wsj.com/articles/BL-MBB-51646.

[102] M. I. Norton and D. Ariely, "Building a Better America—One Wealth Quintile at a Time," *Perspectives on Psychological Science* 6 (2011): 9–12, 56.

mood, which defined an era that found itself torn between wealth and poverty, aristocrats and peasants. French society was organized and managed by the monarchy and its ministers. Approximately 150,000 nobles owned the land and much of the nation's wealth. The clergy totaled about 200,000. They provided spiritual direction for 17 million peasants and a few nobles. This imbalance between the members of the society supplied the necessary conditions for revolt. It acted as a tinder box that burst into revolutionary flames before Charles Dickens captivated the audience when he began his book with these words:

> It was the best of times, it was the worst of times, it was the age of wisdom, it was the age of foolishness, it was the epoch of belief, it was the epoch of incredulity, it was the season of light, it was the season of darkness, it was the spring of hope, it was the winter of despair, we had everything before us, we had nothing before us, we were all going direct to heaven, we were all going direct the other way.[103]

We should analyze this period of history carefully to understand how it parallels modernity. Meanwhile, I know what it's like to live in everyday poverty, and I prefer to live on the other side of this statistic in the best of times. But for now, I abandon myself from the pursuit of fortune for the search of reason.

The prestigious investment houses of Morgan Stanley and Goldman Sachs received approximately $10 billion in TARP funding. In contrast, the Bank of New York Mellon received bailouts that exceeded $3 billion.[104] The Bank of New York and Mellon merger occurred as the

---

[103] Charles Dickens, *A Tale of Two Cities* (New York: Cosmopolitan Book Corporation, 1921), www.loc.gov/item/22004431/.

[104] David Gaffen, "The Bank of Goldman Sachs and Morgan Stanley?" *Wall Street Journal*, September 21, 2008, https://www.wsj.com/articles/BL-MB-4100; Deborah Solomon et al., "U.S. to Buy Stakes in Nation's Largest Banks," *Wall Street Journal*, October 14, 2008, https://www.wsj.com/articles/SB122390023840728367.

financial markets showed signs of worry in July 2007. It is plausible that these two economic giants merged their institutions to survive the Great Recession. They might have been experiencing financial concerns related to their balance sheets, which made the merger mutually beneficial. As a result, government bailouts prevented insolvency. These bailouts also made it more difficult for new talent and businesses to find their way into the market. The doctrine of business as usual manifested yet again. Alexander Hamilton would have been gravely disappointed to learn that the conservative bank he founded in 1784 was now on the verge of insolvency. The bank was now supplicating itself for government assistance to benefit the Bank of New York Mellon.

To avoid this book becoming as dense as *Das Kapital*, I will cite only a few Marxist examples. Corporate behavior has reignited some interest in the earlier ideas of Karl Marx. More specifically, the capitalist actions are reminiscent of Marx's notion regarding inequitable treatment between classes.[105] He wrote about the *alienation of labor* that cut people off from their creativity by isolating them socially with tedious and repetitive tasks foreign to them. He also explained how the worker's production produced wages that were far less than the actual value of their labor. This economic unfairness occurred because the capitalist wanted to extract all the surplus value from their work. As a result, industrial mistreatment led to the hostility between the bourgeoisie and the alienated labor of the proletariat. Marxist ideas promise a worker's paradise but fall short. Every dictator who supported Marxist ideals lived like monarchs and capitalists while preaching the standards set forth by Marx as the people lived in poverty.

My point is that Marxist ideas preach equity and security, which is far from reality. This statement does not justify capitalist behavior, but it is preferred. Capitalists generally feel that they must acquire more income and wealth from all productive means. But unfortunately, this obsession leads to a thinking disorder that compels many industrialists

---

[105] Karl Marx, *The Communist Manifesto* (New York: Penguin Classics, 2015).

to become narcissistic. As their empathy wanes, their self-interest evolves to greater importance. At the same time, the working class responds to these tensions of scarcity for themselves as they demand more equitable pay for their social life. The solidarity of economic interest should create equity in income and wealth among the social classes if such equity is merited. A shortage of income for the worker means they have fewer funds to service their debt obligations. They also have less disposable income to enjoy a culture that makes for a more enjoyable social life.

Worker unions and the minimum wage are often contentious topics of discussion for the capitalist. However, to the worker, the minimum wage allows them to earn a salary that they would not otherwise make. Child labor laws, overtime laws, and minimum wages exist because corporations' natural and historical tendency to procure cheap labor runs deep in our country's history. Criminal wages are no longer possible in this context, thanks to legislation. However, wages are still concerning enough to address here in this space. To combat this wage imbalance, legislators needed to outlaw child labor practices. In addition, they set overtime restrictions before setting mandatory standards for hourly workers' minimum wages. Without these laws, children would work at low wages for corporate titans of industry. In addition, most adult workers would work ten to fourteen hours daily. Working long hours prevented them from obtaining a satisfying social life. Long work hours for meager wages also meant less time and energy to engage with family and friends. Thus, work-life imbalance produced lower degrees of satisfaction in people's lives. To restate this point, legislators cannot trust corporations responsible for economic fairness directed at competitive wages.

Interestingly, if all the corporations offered half the current minimum wage, these wages would be considered competitive. Since the minimum wage is supposed to be a competitive hourly wage for workers, it is still economically insufficient given the cost of medical care, transportation, housing, and food. Periods of inflation make low wages a source of contention for those scraping by. Suppose a minimum wage didn't exist. Workers would make less than the standard minimum wage for their respected states. Although labor unions are not as strong as they should be, they provide a voice for the disenfranchised worker to negotiate better work conditions, including the insistence of a livable wage. If merited, the solidarity of economic interest should create equity for income and wealth among the social classes. A shortage of income for the worker means they have fewer funds to service their debt obligations. It also means that they have less disposable income to enjoy a culture that makes for a more rewarding and enjoyable life.

We turn briefly to business law to understand the corporate structure, which views corporations as people. Mitt Romney responded to a critic in the audience during a presidential debate that "corporations are people, my friend."[106] If corporations are people with individual rights, why allow for socialistic bailouts that defy the fitness rules of natural selection and survival of the fittest? Suppose nature selected a business (individual) to go out of business. The harm does not appear on the failed business injected with a capital infusion. They would continue to use the money on a failing and poorly managed business in this situation. Instead, the other individuals and potential companies find it more challenging to enter the marketplace as the next best economical alternative to fill the vacuum. They struggle to compete with economically failed companies. At the same time, the government resurrects its balance sheets with a capital infusion that provides them with an unfair advantage, and they cite jobs as the main reason for the bailout. Even though most jobs are low-wage earners, they insist on a bailout to perpetuate the status quo. This superfluous economic infusion perpetuates a system of economic nepotism that limits progress.

General Motors is an excellent example because they received a

---

[106] Peter J. Henning, "Treating Corporations as People," *New York Times*, May 26, 2015, https://www.nytimes.com/2015/05/27/business/dealbook/treating-corporations-as-people.html.

capital infusion of $50 billion during the Great Recession.[107] After selling their last shares, the government's total loss to the taxpayer is approximately $10.5 billion.[108] We delay the next generation of innovative companies when we reward failure because of entry challenges. Tesla Motor Company might have emerged much more strongly earlier on if other automotive companies were allowed to dissolve themselves in bankruptcy. With less competition in the automotive sector, Tesla could have risen to prominence more quickly. Instead, Tesla's CEO, Elon Musk, struggled to bring his vision of electric and self-driving cars to the market because there was too much competition. These industrial rivalries should have ended when many of these companies were insolvent. Giving failed companies TARP funding also meant that we would remain dependent on petroleum and companies that couldn't innovate. As seen with General Motors, gas prices are still an issue because of government involvement to keep the status quo.

Post humorously, it is interesting to think about the name of the Tesla company, named after the Serbian American scientist Nikola Tesla.[109] Musk might have foreseen this struggle with Tesla Motor Company, similar to the scientist's fight to bring alternating current to the market. After all, Nikola Tesla's alternating current (AC) mechanism went against his mentor Thomas Edison's concept of direct current (DC), which sparked the "War of the Currents."[110] Edison is not thought about much, even though evidence of his direct current is

---

[107] Neil King Jr. and Sharon Terlep, "GM Collapses into Government's Arms," *Wall Street Journal*, June 2, 2009, https://www.wsj.com/articles/SB124385428627671889.

[108] Jeff Bennett and Eric Morath, "U.S. Remaining Stake in General Mortors," *Wall Street Journal*, December 9, 2013, https://www.wsj.com/articles/SB10001424052748704362004575000841720318942.

[109] Daniel Michaels, "Long-Dead Inventor Nikola Tesla Is Electrifying Hip Techies," *Wall Street Journal*, January 14, 2010, https://www.wsj.com/articles/SB10001424052748704362004575000841720318942.

[110] "'War of the Currents' Had Profound Impact," *New York Times*, February 6, 1979, https://www.nytimes.com/1979/02/06/archives/war-of-the-currents-had-profound-impact-the-war-of-the-currents-had.html.

all around us. Edison is now part of a cherished pantheon of inventors who remains culturally obscure.

In contrast, Tesla is culturally visible and relevant in society. Any company unable to produce innovative solutions has no place in our future when they need a capital life preserver. Suppose a company is too big to fail. In that case, the government should enact the square deal. The square deal could prevent them from becoming too large, especially when these monopolies fail from mismanagement because they are unfit for survival.

The prestige of trickery from our brightest graduates from the best universities destroyed an entire generation of employment opportunities for many people. Their unethical and unsavory approach to business transactions left many people like me lost and riddled with severe economic hardship as we tried to find a new path. Corporate greed had significantly diminished the satisfaction people should experience in a fair and equitable society governed by a philosophy of ethics. Instead, a culture of avarice and arrogance guided their decisions. When leadership disregards the conventional wisdom of ethics as passé and is no longer a valid measurement for success, corporate greed and arrogance manifest as a disruptive force. When rogue corporate behavior disrupts people's social lives for the sake of profit and wealth, it is time for us to redefine our cultural priorities. Our financial markets need to be economically sustainable for the future. Working and living in a capitalistic society when paid like a socialist is not an acceptable course of action that we should tolerate.

I started writing this manuscript after commencement. This book developed due to my own experiences with life dissatisfaction that started early and altered throughout my life. As a result, I focused on how grit and emotional intelligence can affect life satisfaction. My experiences with relearning how to learn and persevere in the face of immense obstacles helped me come to the concept of grit as one of my key fields of expertise. Similarly, self-reflection and effective collaborative interaction were critical themes that helped me engage throughout my life. My career influenced my choice to combine my grit study with emotional intelligence.

When I decided to write this book, I combed through my writing tablets that recorded my thoughts before the recession and afterward. This process helped me remember some forgotten memories and emotions associated with this season of my life. Reviewing many of my journal entries helped with this manuscript. For example, before deciding to return to university, I wrote a wish list about my future career plans in my journal. Some of the items I wrote about included a graduate degree and a doctorate in psychology. I also noted that an exclusively online program was preferable because I worked over fifty hours per week. Since most universities offer hybrid and on-campus programs, I completed my advanced degrees online. As part of my vision, I wrote that I would be a college instructor who would write books while lecturing to the next generation of talented minds.

When times were difficult, I would close my eyes and think about my new career. This technique helped me imagine what my life would be like as a college instructor. It also helped me become more resilient when challenges arose. It provided me with some degree of comfort, imagining what my life would be like as an author and college instructor. It also shielded me from some of these formidable obstacles I confronted in the aftermath of the recession, most of which were related to low wages and credit challenges. While I wrote this journal entry, I acknowledged that these challenges represented a short season in my life. The story of my life is still unfolding in the afternoon of my life. It was up to me to write the narrative to manifest evidence of my vision.

Existential Crisis to Rebirth

The passage of time allows us to view past events with a fresh perspective. People live backward when they gaze attentively toward their past to critique and analyze before thinking about future possibilities. This forethought provides us with a more meaningful understanding of why certain circumstances occurred in our lives and how to make better decisions for a more satisfying future. Enough time has passed to explore my background with a gentle compassion that offers me an opportunity to witness a significant amount of growth. Perhaps this ability to look into my past brings a sobering clarity to my life. It partly helps me reimagine the future from a historical perspective to help me strategically plan my next move.

Like Nietzsche, my struggle with the topic of suffering has evolved in recent years. I now view suffering as necessary to the human condition as water is needed to sustain life. Measurable growth in a person's character emerges from the dark abyss of suffering. Suffering can lead to experiences associated with a renaissance of spiritual and intellectual advancement. This creative mental energy redirects all efforts on a new path of existential meaning. Plucking the roots of dissatisfaction can lead to a new pathway forged from a life wrought with hardship and challenges. A contextual parallel to Frankl's *will to meaning* presents a new path on which man can embark. This *will to meaning* increases generativity and integrity for people to live a life worth living. As mentioned earlier, perhaps Erik Erikson is correct that a life well-lived produces more generativity and integrity. In other words, higher degrees of generativity and integrity lead to more satisfaction because they leave behind a meaningful legacy with fewer regrets.[111] Nietzsche's iconic expression "Whatever does not kill me makes me stronger"[112] is manifested in the art of suffering. Great moments contrasting against profound grief provide deeper meaning throughout the life span. This curious insight allows the person to gaze into the past, riddled with the misfortune of hardship and despair, to a life filled with purpose and meaning.

A nihilistic philosophy plagues the mind. It creates an unhealthy

---

[111] Santrock, *Life-span Development*, 18th ed., 22.
[112] Friedrich Nietzsche, *Twilight of the Idols*, 1889, trans. Duncan Large (Oxford: Oxford Press, 1998), 69.

existential frustration that perverts people's thoughts to believe life is meaningless. This sort of mentality about life is dangerous for anyone to endorse. Life is an adventure that brings many beautiful experiences even though it has some significant challenges we will need to confront. Nevertheless, nihilism distorts the mind's interpretation of events that shackles people to irrational thought processes. These mental schemas distort and cloud their judgment because they are anchored in a philosophy that refuses to acknowledge self-determinism. Frankl states, "Man does not simply exist but always decides what his existence will be, what he will become in the next moment."[113] Freedom to choose one's perspective on suffering can ultimately lead to an inner journey to satisfaction regardless of their current lot in life. Nietzsche's understanding of achieving meaning through suffering led to a more rewarding life. He stated, "He who has a why to live for can bear with almost any how."[114] People should reorient their view of suffering toward a rewarding life that is profitable. Therefore, redirect your suffering with deliberate action toward a direction that transforms the human condition to experience a satisfying and realistic end.

Marcus Aurelius wrote meditations as a private journal that cataloged his experiences and thoughts about various topics. He wrote many of his reflections while traveling alongside the mystical landscapes and the idyllic villages that cradled the Danube River of the Germanic frontier. Famous cities like Vienna, Budapest, and Belgrade sprang up along the Danube many centuries after Roman legions pushed through the Black Forest to the mouth of the Black Sea. Although these regions contributed to music, culture, and Western civilization's neoclassical and baroque architecture that brought us much cultural satisfaction, it is too extensive to talk about in this book. For now, this section ends with the thoughts of Rome's philosopher emperor, Marcus Aurelius, who wrote,

---

[113] Frankl, *Man's Search for Meaning*, 133.
[114] Nietzsche, *Twilight*, 69.

> Do not dream of possession of what you do not have: rather reflect on the greatest blessings in what you do have, and on their account remind yourself how much they would have been missed if they were not there. But at the same time you must be careful not to let your pleasure in them habituate you to dependency, to avoid distress if they are sometimes absent ... withdraw into yourself. It is in the nature of the rational directing mind to be self-content with acting rightly and the calm it thereby enjoys.[115]

Poverty was also a problem for Rome's citizens. Aurelius addressed poverty in ancient Rome while writing in his journal. He said, "Poverty is the mother of crime." When addressing economic inequity, we should always keep his reflection on poverty in mind. Poverty is shameful for any country governed effectively. And any country governed poorly should be equally embarrassed by those who have most of the wealth.

Aurelius also subscribed to the branch of philosophy known as stoicism, which has as one of its primary tenets the view that pain and suffering are part of the journey in life. Although some of the pain can be self-inflicted, we should be stoic in our approach to managing our affairs with grace and dignity. We should interrogate the recesses of our minds daily to transcend our consciousness to a new level. We should also be mindful that troubling events will occur. When they do, we should aim to endure these unpleasantries without showing any feelings that develop into complaining. To say this another way, try not to antagonize your personality with things that harm your nature and muddy your reputation to avoid unnecessary feelings of shame and guilt. Instead, show extreme gratitude for all that you do have, and do not fret about the things you don't possess or the places you wished to experience but didn't. Be silent as you withdraw into yourself, and be

---

[115] Marcus, Aurelius, Martin Hammond, and Diskin Clay, *Meditations* (New York: Penguin Classics, 2006), 172.

satisfied with your decisions. Rather than searching for the short-lived pursuits of fame and fortune in this world, we should focus our energy on nurturing the very things and people closest to us instead of chasing idle and grandiose dreams. Chasing extravagant dreams for the wrong reasons could disrupt the peace of our minds. Instead, we should focus on our mind's harmony, so it doesn't become troubled. While this might appear simplistic, it is not. We should focus on pruning any branches in our garden that don't yield the right fruit. Although this process takes a while, we should not become discouraged since the benefits should produce measurable growth in character and intellect within a few seasons. For these reasons, be patient and "let us cultivate our garden" with deliberate care, as the French philosopher Voltaire wrote in the last sentence of his book *Candide*.

While it will become more apparent throughout the remaining chapters, I am not advocating ignoring or failing to acknowledge your emotions. In its place, I am encouraging the use of the emotional intelligence tool of self-regulation to address them effectively. This idea of suffering as part of life is powerful. It resonates too with my experience of viewing loneliness as a place of refuge and persevering despite the obstacles I experienced throughout my life. As my point of departure, this story ends with the following thought: I would have found it easier to paint a self-portrait of myself on canvas. But on the other hand, I found myself too unskilled with a brush before applying a pen to paper.

While the later chapters of this book include personal anecdotes of how I have experienced passion, perseverance, and consistency, they also discuss how I cultivated these talents through the tools of emotional intelligence and how it is most fitting to position this more extended and overarching narrative alongside my discussion of life satisfaction. These constructs relate closely to my realization that a paradigm shift from an achievement-focused to a life-satisfaction-focused mindset is imperative. It also helps illustrate my expertise personally and scholarly before delving into the novel study on grit and emotional intelligence and how these constructs affect life satisfaction. In choosing to undertake a dissertation on this subject, I was able to reinvent my vocational identity and become an expert on a topic I'd experienced practically for my whole life. I've observed how grit and emotional intelligence helped me complete my university education and how it helped me excel in my first career.

Most importantly, grit and emotional intelligence helped me transition to my new career and identity after the Great Recession. As a result of my collective experiences, I realized the importance of these tools for grit and emotional intelligence. In addition, the underlying attitude shift from the success drive to the satisfaction drive could be helpful in a wide variety of life domains and life stages.

The next chapter details the novel study I conducted on the efficacy of grit and emotional intelligence to address and affect life satisfaction. This academic material established part 2 of this book moves to practical recommendations to apply it in your own life. Finally, it ends with reasons for life dissatisfactions and their effects. This point in the text constitutes a turning point from why life dissatisfaction can occur to how best to address it when it does.

CHAPTER 4

A Novel Study on Grit, Emotional Intelligence (EI), and Life Satisfaction

This chapter reports the novel study I conducted to evaluate the associations among grit, emotional intelligence, and life satisfaction. The existing research considered grit with achievement and gestured only briefly toward the importance of emotional intelligence. Therefore, I decided to undertake a comprehensive study that evaluated grit and emotional intelligence to determine their effect on life satisfaction. This chapter presents a condensed version of that research endeavor and knowledge base. It also identified the need for a new study and the research questions developed for the subject. Finally, this chapter discusses the methods and research design to test my hypotheses, the results, and implications for future research.

At the same time, part 2 of this book is more concerned with the practical applications of emotionally intelligent passion, emotionally intelligent perseverance, and emotionally intelligent consistency. This chapter provides the evidence on which those claims were based. As mentioned previously, there are multiple ways to read this book. While perusing the book in sequence will facilitate the most logical and linear understanding of concepts, this chapter is easily navigable. It has extensive and clear subheadings, so you can refer (or refer back) to it as needed while reading chapters 4, 5, 6, 7, and 8. Before delving into the methods and results of my study, it is first necessary to address the work of previous researchers that led to this point. It is also important to clarify what scholars had not discussed before this research.

Literature Review

This chapter section includes relevant information on several key existing research areas. It was essential to become immersed in the literature before conducting my novel research study. First, I address some of the more historical origins of this aspect of the psychological field, including the development of the IQ scale and early attempts to understand achievement. Then I address the dichotomy with which several researchers have grappled with the importance of innate ability instead of hard work. In the following section, I address other factors that can mediate the effect of grit on achievement and consider the existing literature on emotional intelligence. I also discuss the role of neuroscience and the importance of mirror neurons before considering the issues surrounding self-reporting surveys that have characterized several strands of relevant psychological research. Finally, I address research on life satisfaction in more detail and describe the role of Duckworth's research on grit in inspiring and informing this study.

Achievement Research and the Development of Positive Psychology

While important work on the concept of grit and its role in achievement has occurred in the past decade, there is also a much more longstanding tradition of attempts to understand what makes some humans capable of great achievements. Psychologists have long been fascinated by the factors that distinguish those who achieve great success in their ventures from those who do not. For example, in the late nineteenth century, Sir Francis Galton studied hidden mechanisms of achievement, which led him to create the IQ scale. Galton believed ability, passion, and hard labor to be the common denominators shared by the most successful individuals in any given profession.[116]

In a similar vein, psychologist William James searched for hidden constructs that might help explain the differences between those who demonstrated higher levels of mental volition and those who did not during the early twentieth century. James suggested that psychology focuses on individual differences to explain performance by examining underlying factors contributing to success.[117] Sigmund Freud later explored mental energies, trying to explain the significant accomplishments for a small segment of the population instead of those whose achievements were meager. Freud suggested that this gap between success and nonsuccess was a key reason for widespread dissatisfaction.[118]

More recently, while researchers have continued to search for causal factors that explain or predict performance and achievement, there has been a field-wide shift toward consideration of life satisfaction and other measures of individual well-being. The field of positive psychology has emerged to address those personality traits and other factors that contribute to people's subjective well-being. This broad shift from an achievement-focused measurement system to one that encompasses a more holistic view of what it means to be satisfied with one's life is mirrored in my research. Taking a holistic view of how grit concepts of passion, perseverance, and consistency affect life satisfaction rather than only individual achievement aligns with this shift in focus.

---

[116] Francis Galton, *Hereditary Genius: An Inquiry into Its Laws and Consequences* (London: Macmillan, 1892).
[117] William James, "The Energies of Men," *Science* 25, no. 635 (1907): 321–332.
[118] Sigmund Freud, *Civilization and Its Discontents* (Oxford: Hogarth, 1930).

Innate Ability or Hard Work, and Other Contributing Factors

Many of the first psychologists to address achievement were interested in searching for a mysterious, ineffable quality that leads to success. However, the traits of ability, passion, and hard labor (as Galton suggested more than a century ago) have been supported by recent research much more than theories that feature talent in isolation. For example, as addressed in the previous chapter, Duckworth's concept of grit centers around perseverance and passion, sustained over a long period of time, rather than on a sense of innate ability.[119]

Similarly, perseverance and relentless passion correspond to high performance. That is to say, people who are overachievers demonstrate extreme dedication to an activity, even one that is strenuous and tedious.[120] Gritty people respond differently to stressors. For example, the cognitive conflict they experience because of adversity drives them to higher performance levels, and their intellectual fitness continues to flourish. This form of mental volition and cognitive conflict evolves into a transformative experience for gritty individuals.

Researchers in the psychology field have continued to advance our understanding of the construct of grit as an underlying mechanism contributing to outstanding performance for high achievers across domains. Subsequent work too has found that grit functions as a reliable predictor of performance rather than innate abilities like intelligence.[121] In addition, however, scholars have continued their efforts to clarify other constructs related to grit's effect on achievement and life satisfaction. Some researchers, for example, have suggested that autonomy and competence might function as intermediary agents

---

[119] Angela L. Duckworth et al., "Grit: Perseverance and Passion."
[120] Borae Jin and Joohan Kim, "Grit, Basic Needs Satisfaction, and Subjective Well-being," *Journal of Individual Differences* 38, no. 1 (2017): 29–35.
[121] Angela L. Duckworth et al., "Role of Test Motivation in Intelligence Testing," *Proceedings of the National Academy of Sciences* 108, no. 19 (2011): 7716–7720; Jin and Kim, "Grit, Basic."

for grit and satisfaction.[122] Importantly, this finding suggests that grit is only one of many possible constructs predicting life satisfaction.

Similarly, researchers have suggested extraversion to be a predictive variable for life satisfaction.[123] This variable was also independent of wealth acquisition. Elevated levels of self-control and an improved ability to self-regulate emotions contributed to a healthier self-image, lower levels of depression, and higher degrees of satisfaction. In other words, intelligence is far from the only dimension that explains or predicts success and satisfaction. In addition to grit, the constructs of hardiness and resiliency are critical among individuals who outperform their talented peers.[124]

Emotional Intelligence

Notably, some scholars have used the cognitive construct of emotional intelligence to predict various satisfaction levels. They asserted that individuals who report higher levels of emotional intelligence also tend to report higher levels of life satisfaction.[125] Individuals who can self-regulate emotions, appraise their emotional hygiene accurately, and read the emotions of others around them tend to be happier with their lives in general. As defined in the introduction, emotional intelligence consists of several dimensions associated with emotional competencies and noncognitive aptitudes that enable individuals to respond to environmental demands.[126] The noncognitive competency of grit fits well in this understanding of emotional intelligence because self-reported grit measures require this type of self-reflection.

---

[122] Jin and Kim, "Grit, Basic."
[123] Jin and Kim, "Grit, Basic."
[124] Lauren Eskreis-Winkler, Elizabeth P. Shulman, Scott A. Beal, and Angela L. Duckworth, "The Grit Effect: Predicting Retention in the Military, the Workplace, School and Marriage," *Frontiers in Psychology* 5 (2014): 1–12.
[125] Dana Ackley, "Emotional Intelligence: A Practical Review of Models, Measures, and Applications," *Consulting Psychology Journal* 68, no. 4 (2016): 269–286.
[126] Reuven Bar-On, *Technical Manual for the Emotional Quotient Inventory* (Toronto: Multi-Health Systems, 1997).

More specifically, this study provides evidence for the relationships among achievement, performance, and life satisfaction. These variables are related to particular behaviors that enable individuals to succeed rather than innate abilities such as IQ. My objective in reviewing previous literature was to identify underlying mechanisms that contributed to successful outcomes, including life satisfaction. Previous studies have examined grit to predict satisfaction and achievement. In contrast, other studies examined emotional intelligence to predict performance and life satisfaction. However, the current literature has not examined if grit and emotional intelligence could predict subjective well-being for life satisfaction. Thus, based on the literature review results, I endeavored to understand how the predictors of grit, emotional intelligence, age, and gender affect the criterion variable of life satisfaction.

One of the primary contributions of my study is its intervention in the existing field of emotional intelligence research. Several key elements are instrumental in developing emotional intelligence, first by perceiving the emotions of oneself and then by accurately assessing the feelings of others.[127] As people become more in touch with their emotional states, they acquire emotional knowledge by regulating emotional input and output to foster intellectual growth. The development of an individual's emotions is an appraisal process. To describe and evaluate the quality of both their feelings and the emotional state of other individuals accurately. In other words, possessing a high level of emotional intelligence enables individuals to regulate their emotions and thus increase their self-awareness and awareness of others.

This type of emotional knowledge is necessary for relationship building as well as interpersonal and intrapersonal development. People who use emotional intelligence effectively can self-regulate their emotions. They also tend to be more productive and satisfied with

---

[127] Rosario Cabello et al., "Age and Gender Differences in Ability Emotional Intelligence in Adults: A Cross-Sectional Study," *Developmental Psychology* 52, no. 9 (2016): 1486–1492.

their experiences, especially during challenging life events.[128] These elements are essential for people to navigate difficult obstacles and challenging setbacks to reach long-term goals and be satisfied with life.

Mirror Neurons and Emotional Intelligence

Another interesting and relevant aspect of the literature reviewed for this study was the neuroscientific concept of mirror neurons. Put simply, mirror neurons fire both when an individual performs an action and when they observe another individual performing the same activity. Mirror neurons are associated with acquiring emotional knowledge, learning through observation, and imitation of behaviors.[129]

Concerning emotional intelligence, social mirroring activates specific brain regions associated with emotions. People acquire emotional knowledge by watching other individuals who possess high levels of emotional intelligence. As a result, they can self-regulate their emotions and conduct intrapersonal and interpersonal experiences by imitating those behaviors. Researchers have used functional magnetic resonance imaging to determine if social mirroring is associated with brain regions responsible for emotional knowledge. Such research studies suggest that mirror neuron activity is related to emotional empathy and cognitive empathy levels. Therefore, mirror neurons are relevant to developing empathy, emotion, and social relationships.[130]

---

[128] Ackley, "Emotional Intelligence"; Jeffrey M. Conte, "A Review and Critique of Emotional Intelligence Measures." *Journal of Organizational Behavior* 26, no. 4 (2005): 433–440; P. D. Harms and Marcus Credé, "Emotional Intelligence and Transformational and Transactional Leadership: A Meta-Analysis," *Journal of Leadership & Organizational Studies* 17, no. 1 (2010): 5–17.

[129] Marco Iacoboni, "Face to Face: The Neural Basis of Social Mirroring and Empathy," *Psychiatric Annals* 37, no. 4 (2007): 236–241; Stefan Vogt et al., "Prefrontal Involvement in Imitation Learning of Hand Actions: Effects of Practice and Expertise," *NeuroImage* 37, no. 4 (2007): 1371–1383.

[130] Christine I. Hooker, et al., "Mentalizing about Emotion and Its Relationship to Empathy." *Social Cognitive and Affective Neuroscience* 3, no. 3 (2008): 204–217.

In relation to the association between mirror neurons and life satisfaction, some scholars have suggested that mirror neurons might have developed due to associative learning to foster survival, which is common to natural selection.[131] Thus, the mirror neurons could have adapted to improve the individuals' overall well-being, feel empathy for others, and improve collective survival rates.[132] In addition, such shifts in behavior would have helped individuals predict the behaviors of others, understand the emotional abilities of others, and thereby begin to develop emotional intelligence.[133]

Life Satisfaction

The interdisciplinary study of people's subjective well-being has grown significantly over the past few decades, including scholars from psychology, economics, political science, sociology, and anthropology fields as well as practitioners.[134] Several studies on various topics in these fields have used life satisfaction as an outcome measure, studying the association between independent variables and their effect on life satisfaction. For example, researchers have identified a relationship between academic performance, life satisfaction, positive effect, and adaptive skills. These findings matter because they suggest that such traits are necessary for students to self-regulate emotions and

---

[131] Cecilia Heyes, "Where Do Mirror Neurons Come From?" *Neuroscience and Biobehavioral Reviews* 34, no. 4 (2010): 575–583.

[132] Michaël Dambrun and Matthieu Ricard, "Self-Centeredness and Selflessness: A Theory of Self-Based Psychological Functioning and Its Consequences for Happiness," *Review of General Psychology* 15, no. 2 (2011): 138–157.

[133] Antonella Corradini and Alessandro Antonietti, "Mirror Neurons and Their Function in Cognitively Understood Empathy," *Consciousness and Cognition* 22, no. 3 (2013): 1152–1161; Sashenka I Milston, Eric J. Vanman, and Ross Cunnington, "Cognitive Empathy and Motor Activity during Observed Actions," *Neuropsychologia* 51, no. 6 (2013): 1103–1108.

[134] Ed Diener et al., "Findings All Psychologists Should Know from the New Science on Subjective Well-being." *Canadian Psychology = Psychologie Canadienne* 58, no. 2 (2017): 87–104.

behavior.[135] Through this type of research, scholars have associated more traditional measures like IQ with achievement and overall success, which led to some degree of life satisfaction. In recent decades, however, a paradigm shift occurred. Researchers are moving away from traditional measures like achievement and toward an exclusive focus on the factors that contribute to satisfaction in life. As such, researchers have begun to study a broader array of noncognitive and cognitive constructs that influence areas of human performance and satisfaction.

Emotional intelligence, for example, has been shown to correlate with life satisfaction by positively affecting relationships.[136] People with higher levels of emotional intelligence are more cognitively efficient. They can regulate their moods more effectively. They are faster at retrieving positive memories while in a positive mood, and this outcome contributes to their overall well-being. Several studies have shown life satisfaction to increase with age due to improving relationships and partly because of a reduced pressure to achieve.[137] Researchers reported that higher satisfaction levels were associated with lower incident rates of depression and fewer health problems.[138] In addition, people tended to be more productive at work, and they displayed more positive emotions. This change in their behavior led to a significant improvement in their social relationships, and they tended to live longer.

The gap in the literature led me to investigate the problem associated with low levels of life satisfaction by examining the

---

[135] Susan Antaramian, "The Importance of Very High Life Satisfaction for Students' Academic Success," *Cogent Education* 4, no. 1 (2017).
[136] Joseph V. Ciarrochi, Amy Y. C. Chan, and Peter Caputi, "A Critical Evaluation of the Emotional Intelligence Construct," *Personality and Individual Differences* 28, no. 3 (2000): 539–561.
[137] Tamara Sims, Candice L. Hogan, and Laura L. Carstensen. "Selectivity as an Emotion Regulation Strategy: Lessons from Older Adults." *Current Opinion in Psychology* 3, (2015): 80–84.
[138] Diener et al., "Findings All Psychologists"; Vela et al., *Positive Psychology*.

constructs of grit and emotional intelligence for several reasons. First, after a preliminary search of the literature, I realized that achievement was a dominant outcome measure for much of the research on grit. However, what good is an academic or vocational achievement if an individual does not experience overall satisfaction and well-being in life? This question prompted me to search for constructs relevant to the outcome of life satisfaction associated with grit. Second, further inquiry into the literature revealed that emotional intelligence was central to performance and achievement in specific domains. Lastly, it reasoned that self-regulating behavior for grit and emotions were necessary constructs to reach long-term objectives. Pairing grit and emotional intelligence together meant that people could regulate their emotional responses based on specific settings for a more rewarding life. Therefore, this research is significant to the field of positive psychology. This study could also help researchers gain better insights into the hidden mechanisms related to the constructs of grit, emotional intelligence, and life satisfaction. Additional insights from this study could unearth hidden factors that improve achievement, learning outcomes, and most importantly, life satisfaction.

Angela Duckworth's Work on Grit

Before moving to my study's methodology, it is important to address the most extensive body of work that currently exists on grit. Conceptually, this study owes its most significant debt to the previous work by Duckworth. Her book *Grit: The Power of Passion and Perseverance* includes concepts of grit relevant to this topic and important scales for measuring this construct. In addition, this book attempts to expand on such previous work in positive psychology by assessing how grit interacts with emotional intelligence to produce various degrees of life satisfaction. It also includes practical suggestions for harnessing these constructs to achieve a higher level of life satisfaction.

While the introduction to this book included Duckworth's definitions of grit, it is worth highlighting here the context and basis of her contributions to the field of positive psychology. Duckworth's work on grit has primarily been on the recruits of the United States Military Academy (USMA) and national spelling bee finalists. The USMA used various traditional indices to predict the success of recruits entering Cadet Basic Training (CBT) in the first summer before starting classes in the fall academic semester. Although traditional indices were good predictors of overall cadet success, leadership found that cadets in basic training were quitting their commission before the first academic semester. The standard model of predicting success outcomes at West Point focused heavily on academic criteria. Nevertheless, admission officers soon found such models inadequate as retention rates of first-year cadets continued to decline.

The decline in cadet retention led researchers, including Duckworth, to identify other factors that could better explain success in extremely challenging environments such as the USMA. The Grit Scale provided leadership with another measurement to predict CBT outcomes. The Grit Scale (Grit-O) is a psychometric tool. It uses a two-factor structure to measure the perseverance of effort and the consistency of interest with six statements in each domain from the original study. In other words, studying CBT outcomes makes sense for grit research because of the difficulty associated with the admissions criteria and the individual differences observed among the brightest cohorts of accomplished students while at the USMA. In the seminal study on this topic, researchers examined grit, IQ, and "the Big Five" personality traits (extraversion, agreeableness, openness, conscientiousness, and neuroticism) as predictors of CBT outcomes.[139] The results indicated that grit was a better predictor of CBT than IQ and conscientiousness. Although grit was able to predict which

---

[139] Duckworth et al., "Grit: Perseverance and Passion."

cadets were able to complete basic training, grit was less important as a predictor of cadets' success for the remainder of their time at the Academy. Thus, researchers reasoned that the cadets who advanced beyond basic training to the academic term represented the grittiest group of cadets.

In addition to the Grit-O scale, Duckworth and her colleagues developed the Grit-S measure. This revised scale retained the two domains associated with the Grit-O. It also reduced the number of items to four for each factor to improve the psychometric properties and make the instrument more economical.[140] In addition to the importance of Duckworth's concept of grit to this study, I drew on the Grit-S scale in conducting my research. I took inspiration from the question design for the scales to develop my own reflective questions for measuring emotionally intelligent passion, emotionally intelligent perseverance, and emotionally intelligent consistency.

Research Questions

Based on the literature review, I developed three research questions. These questions hinge on whether grit, emotional intelligence, and two demographic variables (age and gender) can predict an individual's satisfaction with life.

1. Do grit, emotional intelligence, gender, and age predict life satisfaction?
2. What is the unique ability of grit, emotional intelligence, gender, and age to predict life satisfaction?
3. Which variable or combination of variables best predicts life satisfaction?

---

[140] Angela L. Duckworth and Patrick D. Quinn, "Short Grit Scale," 2009, https://dx.doi.org/10.1037/t01598-000.

Assumptions

Based on my literature review findings and understanding of the concepts at play, I made nine key assumptions for this study. The first assumption was that individual differences are responsible for human achievement across domains. Second, I assumed that human performance varies according to success. Many people tend to be dissatisfied with their performance. Third, I thought that not all people have the same level of grit. This idea means that individual differences might account for this phenomenon. To say this another way, I expected to find that grit and emotional intelligence would positively correlate with life satisfaction. I also made sure to account for individual differences in the study design and data analysis processes.

Fourth, I assumed that other constructs (including conscientiousness, deliberate practice, growth mindset, and hardiness) might overlap with grit to explain outcomes. Fifth, I took that the Grit-S could measure an individual's resiliency to life events that allowed them to persevere and overcome challenges. Sixth, I thought that individuals' level of emotional intelligence is variable and therefore contributes to variable life satisfaction outcomes. Seventh, I assumed that grit might be related to life satisfaction. Although these constructs were selected carefully, I designed the methodology to measure them effectively. I also based this study on the assumption that other factors, potentially mediated by grit and emotional intelligence, play a significant role in life satisfaction. As you will see in chapters 5, 6, 7, and 8, I have integrated some of these other factors (of resiliency, deliberate practice, hardiness, etc.) into my recommendations for applying grit and emotional intelligence in the pursuit of your own life satisfaction.

Finally, I made two methodological assumptions when conducting this study. The first assumption was that a multiple regression model would effectively answer the three research questions. Second, this model could measure the relationships between the predictors (grit, emotional intelligence, gender, and age) and the outcome (life satisfaction). It was also assumed that the Grit-S, Brief Emotional Intelligence Scale (BEIS-10), and the Revised Work and Nonwork Life Satisfaction Scale were valid and reliable measurements.

Methodology and Instruments

This study relied on a correlational design to examine the relationship between four potential predictor variables (with two demographic variables included for comparative purposes) and the outcome measure of life satisfaction. The four predictor variables were grit, emotional intelligence, age, and gender. In this correlational study, multiple regression analysis examines the effect of the predictor variables on life satisfaction. In addition, the concepts and scales from previous researchers were reliable and valid to measure the constructs of interest in this study: Grit-S, BEIS-10, and Revised Work and Nonwork Life Satisfaction.

Data Collection

A third-party software company, Qualtrics, provided the services and tools to launch the online survey and integrate the informed consent form and the instruments into a user-friendly, digital platform. After capturing the participants' responses, I exported the raw data and uploaded it into SPSS for analysis. The data collected for this study relied on self-reporting. Therefore, it was necessary to attempt to avoid the risk of bias. In particular, when social desirability bias is present, participants may respond in a manner they feel is socially acceptable rather than providing accurate results. Because of this concern, I implemented several elements into the survey to help reduce social desirability bias. First, all self-reported items were anonymous. Second, the surveys restricted the respondent from viewing more than one item at a time on the screen so they would not be tempted to alter answers after viewing subsequent questions. Third, the respondents could not proceed to the next item in the survey until they answered the previous item and validated their response.

Inclusion Criteria and Demographics

Potential participants were also required to complete several demographic survey items to meet the inclusion criteria. First, they acknowledged that they resided in the United States. Second, they noted that they were between twenty and seventy years of age. In addition to these factors, the demographic questionnaire collects the participants' postal code, gender, race, ethnicity, and level of education. Participants were required to complete all the required fields on the demographic questionnaire before completing the survey. Third, participants needed to speak and read English to participate in the study as part of the exclusion criteria. Finally, since the surveys were digital, not written, they needed access to a mobile device or a personal computer with an internet connection.

The sample consisted of 30.4 percent males ($n = 17$) and 69.6 percent females ($n = 39$). Participants were 39.38 years old on average ($SD = 11.58$). In terms of race, 71.4 percent of participants were white ($n = 40$), 14.3 percent Latino ($n = 8$), 5.4 percent Asian ($n = 3$), and 8.9 percent other ($n = 5$). Of the fifty-six participants, 51.8 percent ($n = 29$) were married, 10.7 percent ($n = 6$) were divorced, and 37.5 percent ($n = 21$) were single. Of the fifty-six respondents, 1.8 percent ($n = 1$) reported having less than a high school education, 21.45 percent ($n = 12$) reported having a high school or GED diploma, 19.6 percent ($n = 11$) reported some college, 17.9 percent ($n = 10$) reported earning an associate degree, 30.4 percent ($n = 17$) reported earning a bachelor's degree, and 8.9 percent ($n = 5$) reported earning a doctorate. Of the fifty-six respondents, 5.4 percent ($n = 3$) were unemployed, 3.6 percent ($n = 2$) were students, 8.9 percent ($n = 5$) were retired, 14.3 percent ($n = 8$) were homemakers, 17.9 percent ($n = 10$) were employed part time, and 50 percent ($n = 28$) were employed full time.

Instruments

This study employed three established psychometric instruments on the survey to assess grit, emotional intelligence, and life satisfaction. As addressed in the Duckworth section of this chapter, similar to the Grit-O, the shorter version of the Grit Scale (Grit-S) can be used to measure individual differences associated with achievement and performance outcomes across a broad domain of professions.[141] The purpose of the Brief EI Scale (BEIS-10) is to assess people's emotional competencies. The BEIS-10 has ten items and is a shorter version of the Emotional Intelligence Scale (EIS), which measured emotional processing with thirty-three items.[142] To develop the BEIS-10, experts assessed the content validity of EIS items for measuring effective content, including emotion, feelings, and mood.

The purpose of the Revised Work and Nonwork Life Satisfaction Scale is to facilitate an overall assessment of how individuals manage their time and energy across the domains related to work and nonwork activities.[143] The work-life satisfaction scale measures respondents' perceptions of balance by assigning a value to ten psychometric items distributed equally across a two-factor structure. The improved work-life balance leads to higher levels of life satisfaction when individuals achieve a balance between work and nonwork activities. Thus, the outcome of work-life balance involves elevated levels of overall satisfaction with one's life.

Conversely, conflict emerges when there is an imbalance between work and life events. Cognitive conflict occurs when there is an imbalance in how people manage their time and energy across dimensions. The Revised Work and Nonwork Life Satisfaction Scale is a two-factor structure with ten items equally disbursed across domains. Based on previous studies that used the same three scales,

---

[141] Angela Lee Duckworth and Patrick D. Quinn, "Development and Validation of the Short Grit Scale (Grit–S)," *Journal of Personality Assessment* 91, no. 2 (2009): 166–174.

[142] Davies et al., "Validity and Reliability."

[143] Matthew J. Grawitch et al., "Examining the Nomological Network of Satisfaction with Work-Life Balance," *Journal of Occupational Health Psychology* 18, no. 3 (2013): 276–284.

all instruments are considered to be reliable (they produce the same results based on the same data each time) and valid (they measure what they say they measure).

Data Analysis

This study relied on multiple linear regression analysis as the most effective statistical calculation for the data analytics process. A regression model analyzes the association between the predictors and the outcome variable based on the three research questions. More specifically, three statistical calculations to evaluate the data: multiple linear regressions, regression of the coefficient for the predictors, and a stepwise analysis.

Results

RQ1

A multiple linear regression tested whether grit, emotional intelligence, gender, and age predict life satisfaction. I used a model summary (see table 1) and ANOVA (see table 2) to examine whether the predictors of grit, EI, gender, and age—when taken as a group—predicted life satisfaction. I found the R^2 value for this calculation to be .32. Therefore, grit, EI, gender, and age account for 32 percent of the variance in life satisfaction, and the model was statistically significant. The results for the first research question show that grit, EI, gender, and age collectively predict life satisfaction ($F(4, 51) = 5.89, p = .001$).

Table 1: Model Summary

Model	R	R Square	Adjusted R Square	Std. Error of the Estimate
1	.562[a]	.316	.262	1.25478

a. Predictors: (Constant), Grit, EI, Gender, Age

Table 2: ANOVA[a]

Model	Sum of Squares	Df	Mean Square	F	Sig.
Regression	37.067	4	9.267	5.886	.001[b]
Residual	80.299	51	1.574		
Total	117.366	55			

a. Dependent variable: life satisfaction—average score
b. Predictors: (constant), grit, EI, gender, age

RQ2

The next research question examined the coefficients of the predictors in the multiple regression in order to determine the unique ability of grit, EI, gender, and/or age to predict life satisfaction (see table 3). Grit ($\beta = .03$, $p = .85$), age ($\beta = .21$, $p = .09$), and gender ($\beta = .06$, $p = .62$) were not significant predictors of life satisfaction after accounting for all predictors. EI is a significant predictor of life satisfaction after accounting for the other predictors ($\beta = .55$, $p = < .001$).

The results for the second research question indicate that only emotional intelligence uniquely predicts life satisfaction after accounting for the other predictors. Furthermore, while the other predictor variables predict life satisfaction when combined, emotional intelligence correlates with life satisfaction even when assessed individually.

Table 3: Coefficients of the Predictors

Variables	B	SE	Beta	t	p-value
Grit	.06	.31	.03	.19	.85
Emotional Intelligence	1.13	.28	.55	4.09	< .001
Age	.03	.02	.21	1.73	.09
Gender	.18	.37	.06	.50	.62

RQ3

The third research question used stepwise regression to discern which variable or combination of variables best predicts life satisfaction. The model only retained the statistically significant predictors. Grit ($\beta = .07$, $p = .58$), age ($\beta = .22$, $p = .07$), and gender ($\beta = .07$, $p = .57$) were not statistically significant, and I therefore removed them from the model (see table 4). Emotional intelligence was statistically significant, $\beta = .52$, $p = < .001$, and thus retained in the model as the only significant predictor of life satisfaction (see table 5). Therefore, the third research question results reveal the only significant predictor of life satisfaction in the model I studied (in isolation) to be emotional intelligence.

Table 4: Variables Excluded in Stepwise Regression

Variables	Beta when included	t	p-value
Grit (Short)	.07	.56	.58
Age	.22	1.88	.07
Gender	.07	.57	.57

Table 5: Variable Retained in Stepwise Regression

Variable	B	SE	Beta	t	p-value
Emotional Intelligence	1.07	.24	.52	4.43	< .001

Implications for Research

This section highlights some of this study's implications for academic research and society at large before transitioning to part 2 of this book. The next part of this book offers a detailed description of how to apply these findings to your own life by developing and harnessing emotionally intelligent grit. In recent decades, the field of study surrounding satisfaction in life has grown to include an interdisciplinary approach that consists of a diverse field of study (including researchers, psychologists, economists, political scientists, sociologists, and anthropologists). As such, this work constitutes an intervention in the scholarly conversation surrounding positive psychology and the role of emotional intelligence and grit in predicting life satisfaction and achievement. Future scholars can build on this work by assessing specifically the effect of different emotional intelligence domains and the emotionally intelligent passion, perseverance, and consistency. Finally, I address the need for society to shift its collective consciousness to life satisfaction as an outcome measure. This shift from achievement to life satisfaction should further advance our academic understanding of these concepts.

In addition, the results have implications for various institutional areas of practice. For example, using these findings could enable organizations and employers to improve workplace conditions and overall employee satisfaction. In addition, increased interest in the importance of life satisfaction as a measurement could improve both organizational outcomes and employees' quality of life. Finally, public and mental health organizations are also domains interested in society's well-being. In other words, if people could improve their well-being, they may feel more satisfied in life, suffer from fewer illnesses, and increase their longevity.

In an educational context, the results of this study could help enhance educational programs that focus on social and emotional competencies to improve students' emotional functioning. In addition, this change in focus would promote more civic engagement and enable students to be more satisfied with life and eventually become more productive members of society. More specifically, these findings could contribute to educational policies advocating for the inclusion of grit and emotional intelligence competencies in school curricula. Overall, the positive aspects of grit and emotional intelligence—including endurance, resilience, perseverance, optimal relationship functioning, deliberate practice, and emotional hygiene—may benefit individuals and society.

Limitations

While this study produced important and novel results, it had several limitations that future studies should address. First, the current study researched a small sample of respondents ($N = 56$). While this sample size was sufficient to ensure statistical power, it was significantly lower than the samples of other similar studies. Therefore, future research should include more participants across a broader demographic spectrum. Second, as mentioned earlier in this chapter, self-reporting may have been an issue for this study's results. Due to social desirability bias, participants may have manipulated their answers to produce more favorable results. Thus, any respondents interested in improving the appearance of their results could have influenced the data by falsifying their responses. For this reason, the respondents could skew the results, exaggerating their performance or accomplishments to feel better about their behavior.

Third, domain-specific skills or contextualization of responses may have improved the accuracy of this study's results. For example, some people do not excel in their profession, but they excel in a hobby. Therefore, their domain-specific scores would be different from their overall scores. As you move into the second half of this book, I advise you to read the advice with a specific domain in mind at a time. For example, you should particularly pay attention to the self-reflective question components of the subsequent chapters. A two-step process might be a good idea. First, feel free to pass through the questions while thinking about their application to your nonwork hobby projects. Second, take another pass to think about their application to other domains such as your parenting style.

Fourth, the items on the surveys were better suited to assessing short-term thinking. This point is important to recognize since long-term durational components are so important to the practice of emotionally intelligent grit. Therefore, future researchers should prompt longer-term thinking among participants in subsequent studies.

Finally, using Qualtrics, I had two options available for collecting the raw data: including or excluding raw data for respondents who did not complete the survey in its entirety. While I elected to include raw data from completed surveys only, this decision could be considered a significant flaw for this study. For example, collecting data only from respondents that completed the surveys could represent the grittiest respondents. In other words, respondents who completed the survey may have been more likely to complete the survey than those who did not have as much grit.

Overall, the results of this novel study indicate that emotional intelligence, in isolation, can predict life satisfaction. Grit too can yield life satisfaction, but only when combined with emotional intelligence. Therefore, the next part of this book focuses on developing emotionally intelligent characteristics of grit: emotionally intelligent passion, emotionally intelligent perseverance, and emotionally intelligent consistency.

PART TWO

Cultivating Grit and Emotional Intelligence to Improve Life Satisfaction

CHAPTER 5

Learning Grit, Expanding Emotional Intelligence

In part 2 of this book, we move into the practical applications of growing and applying different components of emotionally intelligent grit to improve your life satisfaction. First, it is important to establish the underlying premise that grit and emotional intelligence are developable concepts. Then we delve into the separate chapters on emotionally intelligent passion, perseverance, and consistency. It is also essential to let go of preconceived mindsets about these concepts as inherent or innate or that you do not possess, so what is the point? We need to be teachable and open to the experience of learning to be grittier with more emotional knowledge to have a more satisfying life. This chapter aims to present research on grit and emotional intelligence as psychological concepts related to their development. It is also important to note that these concepts are learnable. This chapter also provides some reflective questions and recommendations for assessing and letting go of any existing assumptions that may impede your work in chapters 5, 6, 7, and 8. Further, this chapter's self-assessment and reflection material provide an example of the work you'll be undertaking in the subsequent chapters. These assessment tools provide an opportunity to flex your emotional intelligence to understand your own emotions and mindset.

Social Learning Theory

One of the primary theoretical frameworks in psychology research that applies to learning grit and expanding emotional intelligence is the social learning theory. Developed by Albert Bandura, the social learning theory involved a shift from the focus on innate drives associated with psychoanalytic theory, emphasizing the cognitive mechanisms involved in processing information and their intermediate influence on social behavior.[144] In other words, Bandura suggested a paradigm shift from considering inherent mental characteristics to allowing for how cognitive processes and the environment can affect behavior. Albert Bandura formalized this approach to learning, labeling it the "theory of triadic reciprocal determinism." Put more plainly, this framework allows for the interactive relationship that exists among cognition, behavior, and the environment.

The components of cognition, environment, and behavior are instrumental in shaping cognitive-behavioral outcomes. Most importantly, they are not fixed concepts. They are not permanent ideas, but they are constantly evolving—and, to a large extent, controllable—state of flux. Cognition, for instance, can change on a neuroscientific level. Biological mechanisms can rewire brain structures when different neural pathways are used based on the performance of various environmentally influenced activities. For example, the environment of a rigorous learning environment (like physics and engineering education programs) can cause biological and structural changes in the brain due to the development of new cognitive processes. It follows that such changes in the environment and neural pathways would cause

---

[144] Albert Bandura, "Self-Efficacy: Toward a Unifying Theory of Behavioral Change," *Psychological Review* 84, no. 2 (1977): 191–215, https://doi.org/10.1037/0033-295X.84.2.191.

a change in behavior. In other words, the interchange of the triadic factors associated with the social cognitive theory helps explain how it is possible to develop the constructs of grit and emotional intelligence. There are some key benefits to developing these concepts. First, it helps improve learning and other outcomes. Next, it increases the likelihood of reaching and satisfying long-term goals. Lastly, it helps develop higher degrees of life satisfaction.

For our purposes, the importance of social learning theory and the reciprocal determinism concept Bandura proposed facilitates an important shift in mindset. If, at any point in this book thus far, you have thought something along the lines of *That sounds great, but I'm not a gritty person* or *I'd love to, but I don't think I'm that emotionally intelligent*, this paradigm shift in mindset is a necessary and ideal first step toward the work outlined in the following chapters. Rather than viewing these characteristics as something you have or do not have, you can allow yourself the flexibility to allow for the way your thought processes (which the tools of emotional intelligence can reshape) interact with your environment (of which you can often adjust aspects if it is not working for you) to produce your behavior (which is under your control). Instead of feeling trapped by trait-based personality characteristics, this can enable you to let go of assumptions about what you do not have and move toward understanding and improving the interactions among the way you think, the spaces in which you move, and how you act.

Research on Learning Grit

Several studies have addressed the fact that grit is a learnable concept. For example, one study conducted with a population of professionals from diverse backgrounds found that grit, resiliency, and hardiness were teachable skills across a variety of professional domains (including firefighters, military personnel, and professional athletes).[145]

---

[145] Ralph Brown, "Building Children and Young People's Resilience: Lessons from Psychology," *International Journal of Disaster Risk Reduction* 14 (2015): 115–124.

Researchers asserted that schools and college programs should teach grit, resiliency, and hardiness to both children and young adults based on such findings.[146] Overall, these constructs could improve performance, minimize negative moods, and improve life satisfaction. The concepts of resiliency and hardiness will be discussed in more detail in the following chapters when talking about the tools for cultivating emotionally intelligent grit. Existing research also includes two other concepts relevant to developing grit: the growth mindset and deliberate practice.

Grit and the Growth Mindset

A growth mindset emphasizes adaptability and self-regulation. These characteristics make it a fitting concept that compliments grit and emotional intelligence.[147] A key aspect of a growth mindset involves the perspective that failure is an impermanent condition. If you cultivate a growth mindset, any challenges on your journey to developing emotionally intelligent grit will begin to feel more like learning experiences than barriers.

Several researchers have used the concept of a growth mindset to describe how people can learn to be grittier over time.[148] For example, in her discussion of student performance outcomes, Duckworth discussed the relationship between Dweck's concept of a growth mindset and grit. Duckworth believed these concepts could work in tandem to improve performance outcomes if people were socialized to

---

[146] Brown, "Building Children"; Jeffrey J. Froh, William J. Sefick, and Robert A. Emmons, "Counting Blessings in Early Adolescents: An Experimental Study of Gratitude and Subjective Well-being," *Journal of School Psychology* 46, no. 2 (2008): 213–233.

[147] Carol S. Dweck, *Mindset: The New Psychology of Success* (New York: Random House, 2006).

[148] Angela Lee Duckworth, Patrick D. Quinn, and Martin E. P. Seligman, "Positive Predictors of Teacher Effectiveness," *The Journal of Positive Psychology* 4, no. 6 (2009): 540–547; James J. Heckman and Tim D. Kautz, *Fostering and Measuring Skills: Interventions That Improve Character and Cognition*: National Bureau of Economic Research, 2013, doi:10.3386/w19656.

have higher degrees of grit and a growth mindset.[149] Importantly, and in relation to the social learning theory addressed earlier in this chapter, the proposition that socialization plays a significant role in developing these concepts indicates the effect of environment and interpersonal relationships on the development of effective cognitive processes and behaviors. Other scholars have also asserted that both grit and growth mindset are associated with cognitive-behavioral control networks. In other words, grit and growth mindset are related constructs with a neural connection component. Thus, they can strengthen as the mind works through severe problems. Further, the strengthening of neural networks helps children embrace a growth mindset that encourages the development of the perseverance component of grit.[150]

For the purposes of your work in the subsequent chapters of this book, it is primarily essential to remember that grit is not innate. Since grit is not present at birth, we need to remember that we can nurture this construct. This belief means that this work will be even more efficient and effective by working toward developing growth rather than a fixed mindset. While existing research has already addressed how a growth mindset can work in conjunction with grit, it does not follow that it does not have other applications. On the contrary, I would suggest that cultivating a growth mindset is the ideal first step of this process and the overall purpose of this chapter. Starting from the premise that you are capable of growth makes that growth both easier and more substantial.

Grit and Deliberate Practice

Another variable that researchers often analyze alongside grit is deliberate practice. These constructs are essential to predict

---

[149] Angela L. Duckworth, "Grit: The Power of Passion and Perseverance," filmed 2013, TED Video, 6:01. https://www.ted.com/talks/angela_lee_duckworth_grit_the_power_of_passion_and_perseverance.

[150] Kyla Haimovitz and Carol S. Dweck, "Parents' Views of Failure Predict Children's Fixed and Growth Intelligence Mind-Sets," *Psychological Science* 27, no. 6 (2016): 859–869.

world-class expert performance (spelling bees, chess matches, sports, academics, and music, for example).[151] Researchers have defined deliberate practice as the cumulative amount of time dedicated to a specific activity to acquire skills in a structured environment. This type of deliberate practice has been shown to enhance performance over thousands of hours of effortful rehearsal, usually practiced in solitary environments. While the idea of deliberate practice is often considered in relation to an activity like musical performance, it is also applicable to the deliberate practice of perseverance, passion, consistency, and emotional intelligence. While deliberate practice will be discussed in more detail in the following chapters, it is important to note that each aspect of emotionally intelligent grit can be grown in the presence of a growth mindset and with the use of deliberate practice.

Expanding Emotional Intelligence

Early research on emotional intelligence involved studying factors explaining academic performance among faculty members who were highly intelligent but not very accomplished.[152] Because it became apparent that intelligence was not the only construct to predict faculty members' success, it was necessary to examine the underlying mechanisms for academic performance. This approach helped develop an insightful strategy to evaluate individual differences associated with academics' abilities. These underlying mechanisms proved to be contextual influences that created cognitive conflict and pressures that challenged them and enabled them to grow. More specifically, these challenges led to tensions that helped them develop a broad assortment of noncognitive skills, proficiencies, and

---

[151] K. Anders Ericsson and Neil Charness, "Expert Performance: Its Structure and Acquisition," *The American Psychologist* 49, no. 8 (1994): 725–747; Lauren Eskreis-Winkler et al., "Using Wise Interventions to Motivate Deliberate Practice," *Journal of Personality and Social Psychology* 111, no. 5 (2016): 728–744.

[152] Bar-On, *Technical Manual*.

competencies in the area of intelligence. Notably, the focus on the context in this original research on emotional intelligence means that the premise that emotional intelligence is based on learning from one's environment has been present from the beginning of the academic study on the concept.

Emotional knowledge is necessary for relationship building as well as both interpersonal and intrapersonal development.[153] People who use emotional intelligence effectively can self-regulate their emotions throughout intrapersonal and interpersonal experiences. As a result, they tend to be more productive and satisfied with their experiences, especially during challenging life events. High levels of emotional intelligence also correspond with higher emotional stability and self-regulation. In other words, emotional knowledge transforms the person. More specifically, these qualities of emotional intelligence make obstacles to success and satisfaction less likely to occur. This finding means that these hurdles are not barriers to an emotionally stable person. They are less likely to view adverse events as harmful to their lives while searching for a solution to the problem.

Importantly, this transformative quality means that the possession of emotional intelligence enables people to persist through challenges that are usually disruptive to others who are less able to regulate their emotions. This improved ability to regulate emotions can influence the quality of people's relationships and leadership abilities. Again, by its very definition, emotional intelligence is learned, not innate. This statement means it is impossible to be born with emotional intelligence because inter- and intrapersonal experiences are necessary for its development.

In addition to being a learnable concept, emotional intelligence can help with the learning of other skills. Researchers have asserted that the quality of people's intrapersonal and interpersonal behaviors

---

[153] Ackley, "Emotional Intelligence"; Conte, "A Review and Critique"; Harms and Credé, "Emotional Intelligence."

are essential for developing soft skills. Some soft skills include communication, teamwork, adaptability, and problem-solving, which affect their performance and level of life satisfaction.[154] In other words, people's social interactions provide them with an understanding of how to adjust their behaviors to optimize performance and improve relationships.[155] Social experiences related to interpersonal and intrapersonal interaction are essential to growing emotional intelligence because of the association among thought, achievement, and emotions. Once learned and applied, it is possible to use this emotional knowledge to improve interpersonal and intrapersonal communication. Overall, an emotionally intelligent person uses emotions to make choices about how to think and act in specific settings. Emotional knowledge can build social competence within the community and increase an individual's interpersonal aptitude. In addition, my aim in this book is to suggest that the emotional self-awareness and self-regulation abilities associated with emotional intelligence can improve inter- and intrapersonal competencies and other "soft skills" but also can facilitate the development of passion, perseverance, and consistency.

---

[154] Donald A. Barr, "Science as Superstition: Selecting Medical Students," *The Lancet* 376, no. 9742 (2010): 678–679; Robert M. Kaplan, Jason M. Satterfield, and Raynard S. Kington, "Building a Better Physician: The Case for the New MCAT," *The New England Journal of Medicine* 366, no. 14 (2012): 1265–1268; Gerald Matthews et al., "Emotional Intelligence, Personality, and Task-Induced Stress," *Journal of Experimental Psychology: Applied* 12, no. 2 (2006): 96–107; John D. Mayer, Richard D. Roberts, and Sigal G. Barsade, "Human Abilities: Emotional Intelligence," *Annual Review of Psychology* 59, no. 1 (2008): 507–536; Frederick L. Oswald et al., "Developing a Biodata Measure and Situational Judgment Inventory as Predictors of College Student Performance," *Journal of Applied Psychology* 89, no. 2 (2004): 187–207.

[155] Nele Libbrecht et al., "Emotional Intelligence Predicts Success in Medical School," *Emotion* 14, no. 1 (2014): 64–73; Filip Lievens, "Adjusting Medical School Admission: Assessing Interpersonal Skills Using Situational Judgement Tests," *Medical Education* 47, no. 2 (2013): 182–189.

Evaluating Your Mindset

First, it is crucial to evaluate the extent to which your mindset is currently closer to the fixed or growth end of the spectrum, both with regard to how you view your ability to learn grit and emotional intelligence and in general. As I mentioned in the introduction to this chapter, the next three chapters include reflective questions that enable you to assess your current state concerning each grit concept. Importantly, these reflective questions also benefit from facilitating the practice of emotional intelligence. They provide you an opportunity to evaluate your emotions while moving toward their regulation. The questions to follow are designed to provide you with an opportunity to begin to assess your mindset. These questions should give you a precursor to the type of questions you'll see in the next chapter.

When you reach a section with this type of reflective question, I'd recommend using a notepad or word processor to jot down notes on each. Then allow yourself to spend a bit of time with each question before moving on. After you've completed this exercise, read over your answers before assessing how you feel about them and whether they surprise you at all. Make sure you note any initial impressions for instances in which you identified a solution that doesn't feel functional. And if you suspect a solution will not help you move toward developing emotionally intelligent grit, search for a viable alternative. The answer should always consider how it relates to the concepts of learnable behavior addressed throughout this chapter. Finally, if necessary, begin to strategize about ways to alter or regulate it.

The following questions are designed to help you evaluate mindset (fixed or growth) in a general sense:

1. When you encounter a setback, do you tend to experience a loss of motivation? Or do you move quickly to thoughts of how to move forward from it and of what you'll do the next time a similar challenge arises?

2. Are you more likely to chalk difficulties and setbacks up to situational factors? Or to personal characteristics? ("That was bad luck, but I can do better the next time" as opposed to "I've failed as usual.")
3. When you undertake a new challenge, are you more likely to think first about the knowledge and skills you currently lack or strategize about and experience excitement regarding the ability to grow?

The next set of questions is designed to help you consider the extent to which you currently view grit and emotional intelligence as innate or learnable concepts:

1. When you think about your passions (vocational, hobby related, relational, or in other domains of life), do you consider them fixed and unchangeable? Or do you strategize about how to maintain a sense of interest and purpose over the long term?
2. Do you tend to make statements like "I wish I were more dedicated and hardworking" and—on the positive (but fixed) side—"I have always been a perseverant person?" Or are you more likely to look for ways to become more perseverant and to hone your work ethic and other related skills?
3. When you think about your level of emotional intelligence, do you tend to credit it to personality characteristics? Or do you think about the inter- and intrapersonal interactions that have helped you develop it over time?

Make sure to implement these questions into your life as you move toward the following three chapters. But first, you can apply these questions to different domains in life and essential goals. Each chapter has a series of items or statements designed to move you toward a specific purpose. Second, be sure to return to consideration of these questions any time you feel that you become stuck in a fixed mindset or when you become discouraged. The emotional intelligence, passion, perseverance, and consistency that can improve your life satisfaction are not innate characteristics but can be learned and developed over time. So as you turn to the next chapter, be sure to do so with the underlying assumption that it is within your power to develop your emotionally intelligent passion.

CHAPTER 6

Passion

While the concept of passion generally connotes images of torrid romance and instantaneous, brief forms of emotion, the type of passion that fuels perseverance, is much more longstanding and sustained and—when paired with emotional intelligence—can be carefully, effectively harnessed. In defining the concept for the purposes of her study, Duckworth noted,

> The word *passion* is often used to describe intense emotions. For a lot of people, passion is synonymous with infatuation or obsession. But in interviews about what it takes to succeed, high achievers often talk about commitment of a different kind. Rather than intensity, what comes up again and again in their remarks is the idea of *consistency over time*.[156]

---

[156] Angela Duckworth, *Grit: The Power of Passion and Perseverance* (New York: Scribner, 2016), ch. 4.

Further, she has characterized the type of passion that sustains perseverance and functions as a key element of grit as being marked by "sustained enduring devotion." Importantly, the shift in consideration of passion from implying a short-lived and uncontrollable type of emotion to one that is steady and consistent means that it can be *channeled*. Whereas Duckworth addresses channeling passion for fueling perseverance and producing grit, I aim to address how emotional intelligence tools can be used to channel passion into a form that can be used to produce achievement and a more holistic outcome of life satisfaction. In this chapter, I will address some of the defining points of connection between passion and emotional intelligence, clarify both work and nonwork applications of passion, describe the connection between practice and pleasure as an exemplar of passion, and describe the ways in which self-esteem and self-improvement correlate with passion. Then I will address the measures and potential outcomes of effective and emotionally intelligent passion and provide recommendations for how to channel passion in all areas of life.

Defining Passion: Key Concepts

There are two key differences between passion as most people think of it and passion as I define it for the purposes of this book: the type of passion that can help produce not just achievement in various arenas but life satisfaction as well. First, passion is not a flash in the pan emotion. While it may feel all-consuming, it is also sustainable, dependable, and long-lasting. Second, passion is not uncontrollable. Again, while it might be strong, you can use emotional intelligence tools to channel passion into deliberate practice.

The Psychological Concept of Passion

Since well before the emergence of positive psychology, scholars have attempted to unravel the meaning of success. Researchers in the field of psychology have long contemplated the characteristics, behaviors, and mentality necessary for achievement. In 1892, Francis Galton (half cousin to Charles Darwin) investigated the dimensionality of the mind, which led him to create the IQ scale and measurements for its reliability and validity. Galton studied prominent individuals across a broad spectrum of professions, such as politics, art, mathematics, music, and science. He identified three core traits that produce success: ability, passion, and hard labor.

More than a century later, Duckworth asserted that grittier individuals tend to apply more passion by relentlessly pursuing long-term goals.[157] These individuals also maintained a high level of interest and perseverance. Like Galton, Duckworth studied grit paragons who are experts in their fields and found passion for being a consistent characteristic of their psychological makeup. In Duckworth's grit scale, passion (alongside perseverance) is half of the two-part structure that makes up grit.

Duckworth also delineated key psychological attributes that characterize effective passion and perseverance: interest, practice, purpose, and hope. Of these, interest and purpose relate most closely to the concept of passion. Defining *interest*, Duckworth noted that "passion begins with intrinsically enjoying what you do" and of *purpose* suggested that "what ripens passion is the conviction that your work matters." Building on Duckworth's understanding of passion in relation to grit and achievement, the remainder of this chapter will address how the tools of emotional intelligence can be used to create *emotionally intelligent passion*, which can produce positive outcomes for both success and life satisfaction.

Emotionally Intelligent Passion

Importantly, emotional intelligence tools can take passion from an uncontrollable or obscure emotion to a key driver of action and consequent satisfaction. Emotional intelligence has several possible

---

[157] Duckworth, *Grit*.

interactions with passion. First, emotional intelligence facilitates self-awareness. Before using passion, it is first necessary to identify and understand your own passion. While this might at first seem an easy endeavor, it is an important step that must be undertaken before passion can be channeled. It is vital to reconsider preexisting notions of what passion means and make sure what you're identifying as your passion is actually characterized by longstanding and sustainable dedication rather than brief, strong infatuation.

Further, it is important to clarify which aspect of something you are actually passionate about. For example, maybe you feel passionate about the dream of taking a photography cruise to Norway with your spouse or partner. Before you can channel your passion though, it's important to clarify the aspects of the idea. You actually feel the longstanding passion and parse the dream or goal from the passion that underlies it. Perhaps this particular dream indicates your passion for photography. You think of the cruise as a long-term goal to build by reading books on photography, taking courses, and practicing in your backyard. Or the travel component is the primary source of passionate interest and your passion is related to learning about the Norwegian language and culture. Maybe your passion is for improving your relationship with your partner. The cruise goal is your idea of an ideal bonding experience: time to focus on each other while cultivating your shared interests. Self-awareness then is key in differentiating a goal or dream from the passion or passions that inspire it.

Passion identified, emotional intelligence is the vehicle by which you can use, channel, and grow this passion. Emotional self-regulation and motivation make it possible to use passion to power effort in all arenas of life, maintain consistent practice, and overcome setbacks. In other words, more passionate people are able to overcome obstacles and setbacks in life more efficiently. In addition, they tend to have greater control over their emotional state, which enables them to sympathize with others. Thus, emotional intelligence is also key in helping others identify and cultivate their passions. In parenting, teaching, or leadership contexts, empathy is the key means by which it is possible to help other individuals find and use their passion. For the purposes of this chapter, I define *emotionally intelligent passion* as "self-aware, strong, and sustainable dedication, which can be channeled through self-regulation, motivation, and practice and which can be cultivated in others through empathy."

Passion in Work and Nonwork Domains

Importantly, passion can be used to promote achievement and satisfaction in both work and nonwork domains of life. As addressed in chapter 1, psychological researchers use life satisfaction to describe people's subjective well-being based on their overall satisfaction in life. For example, one study examined work, family, and personal domains—separated into the two domains of nonwork and work—to predict an individual's overall well-being.[158] The authors of that study defined work activities as being related to paid employment, either full time or part time. They defined the domain for nonwork activities as consisting of the family and personal activities important to an individual. The study results showed positive effects of well-being related to both nonwork and work domains. The researchers asserted that an individual's well-being increased when they felt a sense of freedom to make intrinsically satisfying choices. These satisfying choices led to more positive experiences in both work and nonwork contexts. On the other hand, an inability to balance nonwork and work activities contributed to role conflicts and cognitive conflict.

Similarly, another study examined the individual differences associated with life satisfaction in nonwork and work domains.[159]

---

[158] Pam Allis and Michael O'Driscoll, "Positive Effects of Nonwork-to-Work Facilitation on Well-being in Work, Family and Personal Domains," *Journal of Managerial Psychology* 23, no. 3 (2008): 273–291.

[159] Heike Heidemeier and Anja S. Göritz, "Individual Differences in How Work and Nonwork Life Domains Contribute to Life Satisfaction: Using Factor Mixture Modeling for Classification," *Journal of Happiness Studies* 14, no. 6 (2013): 1765–1788.

The researchers aimed to clarify whether individual differences were responsible for the cognitive regulation of both domains, which contributed to the person's subjective well-being and overall feelings of life satisfaction. They reported a sample of working adults ($N = 1{,}704$) who completed their survey. They divided them into two subgroups based on their answers. The first subgroup of adult workers reported equal amounts of life satisfaction across the nonwork and work domains. The second group reported a reduction in the overall level of satisfaction for both domains, but that their nonwork domain produced higher degrees of satisfaction than the work-related domain. The researchers concluded that individuals in the second group were able to compartmentalize the negative effect associated with the difficulties of the work domain. Being able to isolate feelings of dissatisfaction in one of the domains enabled them to feel satisfied with their lives in general. Members of the second subgroup were unsatisfied with their work-related activities. Nevertheless, they were able to self-regulate their emotions in the work-related domain, which allowed them to differentiate work-related feelings from those associated with their nonwork lives.

While this is only a brief foray into extensive academic research on work-life balance and the division between work and nonwork domains, it has a few key implications for our discussion of passion in this chapter. First, it indicates that it is possible to study work and nonwork domains either separately or together in relation to their impact on life satisfaction. Similarly, the type of emotionally intelligent passion addressed in this chapter has clear implications for work, nonwork, or both domains. Further, the results of the study mentioned in this section allude to the key role of emotional intelligence (specifically, self-regulation of emotions) in relation to satisfaction in one or both areas.[160] Finally, we can take this one step further. Suppose self-regulated, emotionally intelligent passion is harnessed. In that case, it

---

[160] Heidemeier and Göritz, "Individual Differences."

can produce positive achievement and satisfaction outcomes for work, nonwork, or both domains.

Practice and Pleasure

One of the key reasons passion is key for promoting success and improving levels of life satisfaction is its relationship to pleasure. Both interest and purpose—Duckworth's psychological attributes that propel grit—help explain how passion can produce pleasure, even within difficult or monotonous tasks. Passion yields both interest in pursuit and awareness of its purpose, through which it can remain pleasurable, even in difficult or repetitive circumstances. While Duckworth views practice as more closely connected with perseverance than passion, other researchers have shown that it can also produce pleasure. And pleasure is necessary for sustainable passion. Importantly, a key misconception about passion is that "you have it or you don't." While passion does, of course, correlate with individualized and inherent interests, that does not mean it cannot be improved, advanced, and sustained through pleasurable and deliberate *practice*.

One study found that grit was related to deliberate practice and life satisfaction because of its association with pleasure.[161] More specifically, hours dedicated to deliberate practice are instrumental in the incremental improvement of skills, which causes the pleasure associated with mastery flow.[162] Peterson, Park, and Seligman suggested that achievement, performance, creativity, and work satisfaction are related to deliberate practice because of the experience

---

[161] Christopher Peterson, Nansook Park, and Martin E. P. Seligman, "Orientations to Happiness and Life Satisfaction: The Full Life versus the Empty Life," *Journal of Happiness Studies* 6, no. 1 (2005): 25–41.

[162] Angela Lee Duckworth et al., "Deliberate Practice Spells Success: Why Grittier Competitors Triumph at the National Spelling Bee." *Social Psychological and Personality Science* 2, no. 2 (2011): 174–181; Katherine R. Von Culin, Eli Tsukayama, and Angela L. Duckworth, "Unpacking Grit: Motivational Correlates of Perseverance and Passion for Long-Term Goals," *The Journal of Positive Psychology* 9, no. 4 (2014): 306–312.

of *flow*. According to the *APA Dictionary of Psychology*, flow—a concept proposed by Mihály Csíkszentmihályi—is

> a state of optimal experience arising from intense involvement in an activity that is enjoyable, such as playing a sport, performing a musical passage, or writing a creative piece. Flow arises when one's skills are fully utilized yet equal to the demands of the task, intrinsic motivation is at a peak, one loses self-consciousness and temporal awareness, and one has a sense of total control, effortlessness, and complete concentration on the immediate situation (the here and now).

In other words, people who engage in the art of deliberate practice are more likely to report higher levels of achievement. They also report higher levels of creativity because they experience this type of flow related to specific, mastered activities, which elicits pleasure. At the same time, this definition is not universally applicable to all kinds of passion-promoting practices. Nevertheless, it illustrates an example of how emotionally intelligent passion, which helps facilitate the peak in intrinsic motivation necessary for flow, can produce pleasure through effort.

Similarly, other scholars have argued that the cognitive constructs of conscientiousness, self-control, and growth mindset enable people to remain focused and disciplined, especially in the execution of complex tasks that demand focused mental volition.[163] Significantly, these emotional intelligence tools can help advance practice and, thereby, sustain interest and promote a sense of pleasure and purpose. In other words, while some of the art of passion is implicit, the tools of emotional

---

[163] Abedrahman Abuhassan and Timothy C. Bates, "Grit Distinguishing Effortful Persistence from Conscientiousness," *Journal of Individual Differences* 36, no. 4 (2015): 205–214.

intelligence—specifically self-regulation and motivation—can be used to further the interest in an activity. It can also help develop a sense of purpose and practice that can make an effort pleasurable.

Self-Improvement

Before moving to the material on how to measure passion, and which outcomes it can produce, and toward recommendations for cultivating and channeling passion, it is important to note the overlap between passion and self-improvement. A drive toward self-improvement can often help differentiate passion from obligation or run-of-the-mill effort. For example, external motivators like money or status can drive effort. Whereas the internal motivator of self-improvement is much more likely to be associated with passion, which can yield effort, that is not a means to an end but an end in itself. Further, self-improvement and resultant self-esteem may mediate the intersection between grit and life satisfaction.

In another study, the researchers examine the interaction between personality traits and cognitive abilities of objective measures related to income, wealth, and personal success. These factors produce positive and negative effect and life satisfaction.[164] For example, they reported that conscientiousness had a significant relationship to satisfaction in life. There was also a medium to a significant association between emotional stability and life satisfaction. However, they found no association between income and wealth. Most importantly, they found self-esteem to be a mediating factor between grit and life satisfaction. Similarly, other researchers have suggested that self-improvement and emotional intelligence were related to life satisfaction.[165] Based on those results, alongside the

---

[164] Angela L Duckworth et al., "Who Does Well in Life? Conscientious Adults Excel in Both Objective and Subjective Success," *Frontiers in Psychology* 3, (2012): 356–363.

[165] Benjamin Palmer, Catherine Donaldson, and Con Stough, "Emotional Intelligence and Life Satisfaction," *Personality and Individual Differences* 33, no. 7 (2002): 1091–1100.

findings of the novel study presented in chapter 4 of this book, it is possible to suggest that passion—partially through its relationship to self-improvement and role in producing improved self-esteem—can be key in promoting life satisfaction.

My Experience with Passion

The best example of passion I've experienced in my life is the sustained interest I worked hard to cultivate throughout my PhD process. While those who have not completed a doctoral degree may imagine a bright-eyed graduate student leisurely reading books they enjoy and jotting down their thoughts on the subject, the process is—as I mentioned in chapter 2—marked by academic hazing and intense difficulty. In comparison, most PhD students *begin* the process with the type of passion for the subject that we view as a more traditional iteration of the concept of love and enjoyment. I can assure you that any "bright-eyed" and passionate interest, at least in that sense, does not persist. During the process of writing a dissertation, most graduate students actually come to hate their subject matter, at least for a period of time, by virtue of having spent such an inordinate amount of time with it. How then did I learn to sustain the passion required to complete the degree?

Before becoming a psychologist, I viewed passion as a short-term interest associated with something loved and wanted for the moment. I didn't think that suffering could be part of the passion experience or of passion as something that required a degree of effort (sometimes a great deal of effort) in order to be maintained. This insight into passion developed throughout my doctoral experience. Writing a dissertation is not an easy task. Creating a tome consisting of hundreds of pages is difficult enough in the abstract. Add to that the fact that it must contribute something *completely new* to existing knowledge, the fact that advisors and committee members all have their own view on how it should be written, the fact that new research and events that affect one's argument are emerging all the time, as well as the normal issues like finding the time to write as a graduate student and experiencing writer's block. It becomes something that seems almost insurmountable. There were many times that I wanted to give up, but I didn't. I remember thinking that I set a goal to finish the program, and I needed to figure out how to suffer through the rigor of the writing process.

The complex nature of writing requires effort, time, and perseverance. It is a marathon of grit that requires some emotional knowledge that assisted me in writing. Of course, I couldn't get the project done in a single weekend. Therefore, I adhered to a strict writing schedule. My manuscript demanded attention daily so that I could read journal articles about my research topic and books. To manage my time for reading and writing, I maintained a deliberate practice journal. The journal recorded how many hours I worked on the project. It also provided me with weekly and monthly totals, and it helped me become consciously aware of how I spent my time. This awareness helped me cultivate a deliberate action that pushed me to work for a long stretch of time, even though it was not enjoyable. It helped me learn how to manage my time more efficiently and tune out many of the distractions that interfered with this creative process. In relation to passion, even when my interest in the subject matter waned for some time, my interest in and drive to accomplish my writing goals helped carry me through the process.

I also learned that I needed to prioritize activities in my life that weren't related to writing. These priorities meant fewer social activities with friends and less time interacting with content on social media. I also restricted television time until I reached my daily objectives. These changes conditioned me to work for more extended periods. Life often got in the way of the writing process because of the lengthy commitment needed to finish. I remember many instances when emotions disrupted my flow. I needed to learn how to manage these disruptions by learning how to compartmentalize emotions, but this took time. Eventually, I learned how to deal with any obstacle that gets in the way at a later time, a process that I'll discuss in more detail in the following chapter concerning perseverance.

Importantly, my experience of passion was rarely enjoyable, except when I succeeded in completing each milestone I set (a chapter, a page, or at times even just a sentence). An asceticism to passion has the potential to make you feel obsessed about an activity that is important to you, even if it doesn't accompany much enjoyment. There were many occasions when I felt distant from or even resentful about my work and subject matter. I pored over articles and books about it for countless hours while painstakingly writing and rewriting the same sections of text over and over again. Often, I had to try to remind myself of its implications and my interest in it.

Nevertheless, my experience was interesting and unique, given that I was writing about the very things that enabled me to continue writing: grit. Even when things were difficult, I was aware that the tools of grit and emotional intelligence I was writing about had helped me through the most difficult times in my life, and they would eventually be able to help others too. As Duckworth noted, purpose is connected to passion, and I tried to remain aware that my purpose was to discover new knowledge about this subject and eventually be able to share it with others in the hope that it would be an asset to them in their own lives, as it was to me.

Writing my dissertation required thousands of hours of sustained passion. Although my writing was often terrible in its first iteration, it improved substantially with each successive rewrite. I found myself revising my work even when I didn't want to. Instead, I remembered to check in with myself and redirect my thoughts using emotional intelligence tools. This process enabled me to sustain the passion, interest, and a sense of purpose I needed, even when those feelings were offset by those of dislike, fatigue, pain, and suffering.

Measures/Outcomes
Grit-Scale Passion Measures

Given that passion is a fairly abstract concept, it does promote some measurement challenges. More specifically, it is only possible to measure passion through self-reported, internal reflective measures rather than any external metric. On Duckworth's grit scale, which asks individuals to rate themselves on a scale from a 5 (not at all like me) to a 1 (very like me), the odd-numbered questions are those explicitly related to passion.

1. New ideas and projects sometimes distract me from previous ones.
3. I often set a goal but later choose to pursue a different one.
5. I have difficulty maintaining my focus on projects that take more than a few months to complete.
7. My interests change from year to year.
9. I have been obsessed with a certain idea or project for a short time but later lost interest.

To determine your score for perseverance, add the answers and divide by 5 to determine the passion element of your grit score (with 1 being the lowest and 5 being the highest). While this chapter or book aims not to develop a scale, like Duckworth's, for measuring emotionally intelligent grit, it is worth proposing several questions that can help facilitate self-awareness regarding passion. And as mentioned in the previous section, because self-awareness is a key aspect of emotional intelligence through which you can identify and grow passion, the very act of engaging in this type of self-reflection can be useful in terms of promoting tools for understanding your own passion and the degree to which it is emotionally intelligent.

Measuring Emotionally Intelligent Passion

As mentioned previously in this chapter, self-awareness is key in identifying and understanding your own passion. As such, the following questions are designed to help you measure the extent to which you understand your own passion:

1. Do you characterize your passion or passions as a part of your identity?
2. Do you have difficulty differentiating your *passions* from your goals or dreams?
3. Can you parse aspects of performing your passion, differencing those you enjoy in their own right from those you tend to consider a means to an end?

Similarly, thinking about answers to the following set of questions can help you develop your understanding of the extent to which you are able to use and channel your passions through the tools of emotional intelligence:

1. Would you define your passion and the way you pursue it as self-regulated or haphazard?
2. Do you often experience a lack of motivation to pursue your passion?
3. Are you able to use self-motivation to overcome obstacles associated with pursuing your passion?

Finally, the following questions are related to the areas of helping other people (employees or one's children, for example) cultivate and use their passions:

1. Would you characterize yourself as having an empathic understanding of other people's passions, even when they do not overlap with your own?

2. Do you tend to be able to identify other people's passions through their actions, even when they haven't explicitly told you about them?
3. Are you comfortable offering advice and guidance to others about how to grow, sustain, and use their passion?

Again, while it is not my aim that these passions should function as a scale through which to measure emotionally intelligent passion precisely, they do provide a useful tool through which you can develop a more reflective and self-aware understanding of passion. Therefore, while I have addressed potential outcomes of effective passion throughout this chapter, and while cultivating your own passion will produce unique outcomes specific to you, it is worth returning to my definition of emotionally intelligent passion in order to frame some of the positive outcomes that can result from cultivating this type of passion: *self-aware, strong, and sustainable dedication, which can be channeled through self-regulation, motivation, and practice and which can be cultivated in others through empathy.*

Passion Facilitates the Shift from Interest to Purpose

First, self-awareness concerning passion helps facilitate a shift from interest to purpose. Whereas interest is associated with the enjoyment of the endeavor about which you are passionate, purpose helps orient your efforts toward your *why*: the broader implications of your passion. Importantly, these implications are as variable as passions themselves. Even so, a positive outcome of self-aware passion is that it can help you develop more clarity and nuance in relation to both interest and purpose.

Passion Sustains Effort

Second, emotionally intelligent passion—and the self-aware sense of interest and purpose it entails—can help sustain your effort over time.

When coupled with self-regulation and motivation, passion will help you overcome challenges met and ride out lulls in progress. Here, it is worth pausing to note that passion is characterized by sustained dedication. It does not mean that you are likely to experience the same level of stamina each day. While it can look this way, passion does not mean that you leap from bed before dawn every single day, excited to pursue your passion. It rarely works this way. Instead, you should expect adversity, and when it happens, plan to modify your effort to stay on track. The events in life can sometimes be an obstacle when faced with unwanted circumstances or internal struggles that force you to mitigate action. Nevertheless, you can retain your drive toward the aim of your long-term passion and accomplish small steps toward it even when energy levels are low.

Further, passion underlies the consistent daily practice needed to grow your grit and emotional knowledge. Although deliberate practice requires continual effort, it can sometimes feel monotonous because of the lack of variety. However, the daily repetition can also yield flow, mastery, and the achievement of long-term goals. Again, emotionally intelligent passion allows for some variation in an effort that ensures intrinsic motivation. This variation in effort means that you can consciously promote the use of self-regulation tools to nurture passion.

Passion Begets Passion

Finally, understanding and cultivating your passion can help you become a better leader, boss, partner, teacher, or parent. More specifically, it can equip you to help others identify and use their passions as well. Through the tools of empathy, emotionally intelligent passion can help unearth and grow emotionally intelligent passion in others.

Growing Emotionally Intelligent Passion

As I have alluded to throughout this chapter, it is important to remember that passion is not limited to either work or nonwork domains or toward macro or micro aspects of life. Passion can as easily be tied to a broad, career-spanning ambition as to a personal and internal nonwork arena. While this section will offer general recommendations, they are applicable to various domains in which passion can operate.

Deliberate Practice Journal

Because the self-awareness component of emotional intelligence is so crucial to cultivating passion, developing tools for self-reflection is paramount. One form this can take is a deliberate practice journal. To use this tool, think and write through the questions presented earlier in this chapter or on subjects associated with different elements included in the definition of emotionally intelligent passion identified earlier. First, identify your passion. What are you passionate about? Is it part of a work or nonwork domain of life? Which elements comprise it? What are the goals and outcomes with which you associate it? Second, think about how you're growing your passion and how you can advance these aims. What goals have you set to work on your passion in the short, medium, and long term? How do you overcome challenges or obstacles to your passion? How could you do this better? These tools allow for the type of self-regulation that will help you advance your passion.

Finally, think about the outcomes of your passion. What do you hope to achieve in your passion? What satisfaction will it yield? Identifying the *key outcomes* of your passion will help you course-correct when things become difficult. We should remember that key results can range from personal contentment to high-level career achievement. Importantly, this does not have to take the form of a paper-and-pen journal. Be sure to play to your strengths and build your self-awareness of passion in the same way you work through other critical thought exercises.

If writing, for example, is not the most helpful tool for you, your deliberate practice journal could take the form of conversations with a friend, family member, or colleague. You can then talk through your answers to these questions aloud. Another example instead of writing is drawing a caricature of something you feel passionate about in your life. You can sketch portraits, pictures, and cartoons instead of writing. Drawing caricatures of the way you feel could produce the unintended consequence of writing. Perhaps, drawing can inspire a short burst of writing to express the cartoons more clearly.

Finally, you can use a deliberate practice journal to tell stories qualitatively. However, deliberate practice journals can also record data quantitatively. It can record the number of hours spent practicing a given activity toward developing emotionally intelligent passion. For instance, knowing how many hours you write is vital to an inspiring writer. Perhaps you learn that you write three to six hours a day because you record daily activities in your deliberate practice journal. The idea is to quantify the writing daily, weekly, monthly, and annually. As you log more hours writing, your flow and prose improve. Before you know it, you have a finished manuscript ready for publication.

Similarly, to help facilitate others' emotionally intelligent passion, find tools to encourage self-reflection and use them. For example, either parenting or education settings can use self-reflection to promote exploration, experiential learning, and creative projects. This form of encouragement can enable young children to think about their passions. Perhaps another example is a leader who intends to develop employees' emotionally intelligent passion in a workplace context. The leader includes a self-reflection requirement in quarterly evaluations to achieve this objective. In addition, the team leader might schedule one-on-one conferences or team meetings with space for individuals to reflect on their passions. As a result, the employee begins to make structural changes to their decisions to boost productivity and satisfaction levels while working.

Blend Effort and Play

As extant research illustrates, practice can promote pleasure and mastery, a state of flow.[166] While the idea of the flow state is not applicable to all types of passions, it does offer a vital directive: hard effort and playfulness both have a role in cultivating passion. Furthermore, all passions entail difficult or tedious moments as well as triumphant and enjoyable ones. Therefore, it is essential to self-regulate by becoming aware of a stumbling block or waning of motivation. This way, you can respond by shifting to a more enjoyable aspect of the task or returning to the parts of the passion you first became interested in pursuing.

The idea of play is particularly applicable to cultivating passion in one's children or students. Encouraging enjoyment of a passion enables young people—and indeed, all of us—to persist in a task by becoming acquainted or reacquainted with the parts of it we find most intriguing and fun. This fact is as true of a child's burgeoning interest in music—through a saucepan orchestra—as it is of the workings of an elite mathematician. Finding play within effort and fun within a more complex and enduring passion is essential to its maintenance.

In addition to pairing passion with perseverance to produce achievement, it can yield higher levels of life satisfaction when combined with emotional intelligence. The tools of emotional intelligence—specifically self-awareness, self-regulation, motivation, and empathy—can be used to identify, advance, and sustain passion in both self and others. While I have suggested the longstanding nature of passion, I will delve more deeply into the concept of consistent, continual effort in the following chapter. The next section addresses the reasons for cultivating and ways to grow emotionally intelligent perseverance.

---

[166] Peterson et al., "Orientations to Happiness."

CHAPTER 7

Perseverance

Passion already connotes widespread applications throughout an individual's social, leisure, relational, and work-life and thus connects readily with the concept of life satisfaction. However, perseverance is usually associated with achievement rather than satisfaction. Suppose the constructs of perseverance and satisfaction run concurrently. In that case, it is often in the sense of perseverance having yielded a satisfying (usually work- or goal-related) outcome rather than satisfaction in its own right. It is understood not as a satisfying practice but as a tool to ensure achievement. However, if we reconceptualize perseverance—and in particular if we practice *emotionally intelligent* perseverance—it becomes clear that consistent perseverance can yield a continually satisfying journey as well as arrival at one's intended destination.

In this chapter, I first address the definition of perseverance in relation to the concept of resilience, which is a key aspect of how perseverance can produce life satisfaction not just through positive outcomes but through a continual process of countering obstacles. Then I address the concept of emotionally intelligent perseverance before defining it with emotional stability and self-regulation concepts. The following section addresses the measures and potential outcomes of perseverance, moving from Duckworth's existing scales to new standards for, and possible effects of, emotionally intelligent perseverance. Finally, I provide practical recommendations for persevering in an emotionally intelligent manner throughout diverse domains of life.

Resilience and Perseverance

We must shift our paradigm to understand resilience as an *end* that produces life satisfaction. This change occurs through associated accomplishments that harness it as a continual *means* by which individuals can experience consistent satisfaction when overcoming obstacles. Thus, the concept of resiliency becomes important to perseverance. While, as addressed in the previous chapter, Duckworth's attributes of interest and purpose are closely related to the concept of passion, those of *practice* and *hope* are key types of perseverance. For example, suppose the practice of an activity is related to perseverance. In that case, it is because of "the daily discipline of trying to do things better than we did yesterday."[167] This discipline is a drive toward a "focused, excited, challenge-exceeding-skill practice that leads to mastery." In addition to this day-to-day expression of perseverance, Duckworth addressed hope as a "rising-to-the-occasion kind of perseverance," which is closely related to the concept of resilience.

Resiliency and perseverance are close cousins to emotional intelligence. However, before we frame resiliency to grit, it is fitting to delve more deeply into the concept of resilience related to grit, emotional intelligence, and life satisfaction. According to the *APA Dictionary of Psychology*, resilience is

> [T]he process and outcome of successfully adapting to difficult or challenging life experiences, especially

---

[167] Duckworth, *Grit*, ch. 5.

through mental, emotional, and behavioral flexibility and adjustment to external and internal demands. A number of factors contribute to how well people adapt to adversities, predominant among them (a) the ways in which individuals view and engage with the world, (b) the availability and quality of social resources, and (c) specific coping strategies. Psychological research demonstrates that the resources and skills associated with more positive adaptation (in other words, greater resilience) can be cultivated and practiced.

This definition is essential for the objectives of this chapter in several ways. First, it addresses the importance of the *process* as well as the outcome. Second, concerning perseverance, resilience is the characteristic by which individuals can engage in the consistent practice of overcoming obstacles. Further, the definition relates specifically to the concept of emotional flexibility and "adjustment to external and internal demands," both of which are key expressions of emotional intelligence. Finally, this definition highlights the belief that resilience is not an innate construct. People are not born with the ability to be resilient or with the talent to persevere through obstacles, which means our experiences nurture these constructs.

Similarly, researchers noted that individuals learn to build resiliency when faced with adversity; this process of coping with adversity helps develop healthy functioning, which is an underlying mechanism for perseverance.[168] This concept—of resilience as an underlying mechanism for perseverance—is crucial for this discussion. Before moving to the following section, it is necessary to address several concepts researchers have frequently associated with resilience: hardiness and a growth mindset.

---

[168] Adam J. Vanhove et al., "Can Resilience Be Developed at Work? A Meta-Analytic Review of Resilience-Building Programme Effectiveness," *Journal of Occupational and Organizational Psychology* 89, no. 2 (2016): 278–307.

Hardiness

Several scholars have addressed the concept of resiliency with grit and hardiness. As mentioned in the previous chapter, a study with professionals from diverse backgrounds found that grit, resiliency, and *hardiness* were teachable skills.[169] Further, the study showed that these constructs were partly responsible for higher levels of performance. They also have the power to minimize negative moods and improve life satisfaction.

Similarly, another study was conducted with bank managers to examine if grit and hardiness could predict employees' health, performance, and satisfaction.[170] They reported that, in conjunction, grit and hardiness could predict their levels of resiliency. They also said that higher degrees of grit and hardiness (and consequent resiliency) led to better health, increased performance, and higher degrees of satisfaction. The researchers asserted that hardiness helps individuals perform better in stressful situations because hardy people tend to evaluate demanding threats as an opportunity to do something constructive. As will be discussed in the potential outcomes section of this chapter, emotionally intelligent perseverance can have a similar effect in terms of reframing individuals' understanding of obstacles as opportunities for short-term satisfaction and success.

Growth Mindset

Scholars have also associated the development of resiliency with the presence of a growth mindset. Dweck identified two types of prevalent mindsets: a *fixed mindset* and a *growth mindset*.[171] Dweck characterized the latter as being exemplified by an emphasis on adaptability and self-regulation. Individuals who embrace a growth mindset are more

---

[169] Brown, "Building Children."
[170] Vishal Ghule and B. R. Shejwal, "The Role of Cognitive Hardiness in Health and Performance of Bank Managers," *Indian Journal of Health and Wellbeing* 7, no. 4 (2016): 383.
[171] Dweck, *Mindset*, 6.

likely to realize that failure is not a fixed condition but a malleable one. In relation to grit and perseverance, researchers suggested that grittier individuals learn to build resiliency when confronted with adversity because they have a growth mindset rather than a fixed mindset; further, this type of resiliency promotes healthy cognitive functioning.[172] In other words, resiliency is essential because it helps individuals maintain focus during moments of adversity.

Another study suggested both grit and growth mindset to be associated with cognitive-behavioral control networks.[173] In other words, grit and growth mindset are related constructs that might have a neural connection. Similarly, other researchers made the following three observations: emotional intelligence and subjective well-being are correlated, positive attitudes and selfless behavior contributed to subjective well-being, and with elevated levels of emotional intelligence exhibited higher levels of resiliency.[174] Further, Dweck noted that a growth mindset is essential for both resilience and the self-regulation of pliable emotions.[175] This finding suggests that key concepts associated with perseverance—resilience, hardiness, and growth mindset—require emotional intelligence for their cultivation and practice. As the next section will show, the regulatory tools of emotional intelligence are imperative in the development, harnessing, and sustainment of perseverance.

---

[172] Duckworth, "Grit"; Duckworth, *Grit*; Deborah Perkins-Gough and Angela L. Duckworth. "The Significance of GRIT: A Conversation with Angela Lee Duckworth." *Educational Leadership* 71, no. 1 (2013): 14–20; Vanhove et al., "Can Resilience Be Developed at Work?"

[173] Chelsea A. Myers et al., "The Matter of Motivation: Striatal Resting-State Connectivity Is Dissociable between Grit and Growth Mindset," *Social Cognitive and Affective Neuroscience* 11, no. 10 (2016): 1521–1527.

[174] Jiatao Huang, Hongbo Shi, and Wei Liu, "Emotional Intelligence and Subjective Well-being: Altruistic Behavior as a Mediator," *Social Behavior and Personality* 46, no. 5 (2018): 749–758.

[175] Dweck, *Mindset*.

Defining Emotionally Intelligent Perseverance

Researchers have asserted that individuals who possess higher degrees of grit tend to be more cognitively aware of themselves.[176] People who are more cognitively aware of themselves, in turn, are more likely to identify conflicts that exist internally and externally. Thus, being cognitively aware of themselves is an essential feature of grit and conflict resolution. It could prompt them to seek a resolution by identifying the causes of these conflicts. In relation to perseverance, concepts of emotional intelligence are key in that—when faced with adversity (or upon seeing someone else faced with adversity)—they enable us to understand, regulate, engage with, and redirect the negative emotions associated with obstacles and challenges.

In a more general sense, psychologists have addressed concepts of emotional intelligence to emotional knowledge acquired through intrapersonal and interpersonal relationships. Emotional intelligence scholars have defined the concept as a cognitive trait measured across five dimensions.[177] The first dimension measures individuals' capacity to comprehend their emotions. The second factor appraises their ability to accurately evaluate the feelings of others with whom they interact. The third dimension measures individuals' ability to regulate their emotions by seeking out stimuli that make them happier. This ability to regulate their emotion is essential to their happiness because it allows them to feel more empowered while controlling their feelings. The fourth element measures the individuals' ability to regulate the emotions of others. The fifth component measures if people could use positive emotions to develop new ideas during challenging moments when obstacles present challenges to sustained productivity.

While discussing perseverance, the third and fifth dimensions of emotional intelligence are particularly important. When people are able to regulate their emotions through redirecting their thoughts, it is

---

[176] Grawitch et al., "Examining the Nomological Network."
[177] Davies et al., "Validity and Reliability."

more likely that they can sustain—and even derive pleasure from—the process of overcoming obstacles. Similarly, the fifth dimension's focus on creating new ideas through the use of positive emotions in the face of obstacles suggests that adding emotional intelligence to perseverance can yield both positive emotion and creativity.

Indeed, researchers have found that people who used emotional intelligence effectively were able to self-regulate their emotions throughout intrapersonal and interpersonal experiences. As a result, they were more productive and satisfied with their experiences, especially during challenging life events. High levels of emotional intelligence also correlate with more emotional stability and self-regulation. Emotional intelligence built more stable personalities that enabled people to persist through much more disruptive challenges to those who cannot regulate their emotions. Researchers have found that successful performance outcomes are related to grit and resiliency.[178] It appears that the grittier and more resilient you are, the more likely you can adapt to adversity while self-regulating your emotions. In this way, emotionally intelligent perseverance can contribute to both performance and life satisfaction.[179]

This point needs more detail of which the next section discusses. Before providing a novel definition of *emotionally intelligent perseverance*, we turn to the relationships between emotional stability and perseverance and self-regulation and perseverance.

Emotional Stability

According to the *APA Dictionary of Psychology*, emotional stability is defined as "predictability and consistency in emotional reactions, with an absence of rapid mood changes." In terms of overcoming

---

[178] Jaclyn M. Stoffel and Jeff Cain, "Review of Grit and Resilience Literature within Health Professions Education." *American Journal of Pharmaceutical Education* 82, no. 2 (2018): 6150-134.
[179] Barr, "Science as Superstition"; Kaplan et al., "Building a Better Physician"; Matthews et al., "Emotional Intelligence."

obstacles, emotional stability is particularly important in relation to the ability to understand and manage the emotions associated with facing challenges. According to the developers of the basic emotional intelligence scale, students who employed tools based on this scale could self-regulate their behavior more effectively within the setting of a learning environment because they were able to appraise their emotions and the feelings of others to improve behavioral outcomes.[180] Similarly, in their study on subjective perceptions of life satisfaction, Vela and colleagues determined that grittier people could better comprehend and manage their emotions.[181] They found that understanding both their own and others' emotions correlated with individuals' ability to adapt their behavior to changing environmental situations. Importantly, concerning perseverance, emotional stability does not mean that individual experiences are only positive emotions upon facing challenges. Instead, it means that individuals who exhibit emotionally intelligent perseverance can calmly identify, mitigate, and redirect negative emotions. As a result, they are less likely to be derailed by obstacles because they are more likely to retain composure while working toward a solution.

Self-Regulation

According to the *APA Dictionary of Psychology*, self-regulation can be defined as "the control of one's behavior through the use of self-monitoring (keeping a record of behavior), self-evaluation (assessing the information obtained during self-monitoring), and self-reinforcement (rewarding oneself for appropriate behavior or for attaining a goal)." Concerning grit, both Duckworth and other scholars recommended that future researchers should examine the combination of grit and

---

[180] Davies et al., "Validity and Reliability."
[181] Vela et al., "Positive Psychology"; Javier C. Vela et al., "The Impact of Individual, Interpersonal, and Institutional Factors on Latina/o College Students' Life Satisfaction," *Journal of Hispanic Higher Education* 15, no. 3 (2016): 260–276.

emotional intelligence. This suggestion is because both traits require people to self-regulate their emotions.[182] For example, suppose emotional stability is associated most readily with identifying and managing negative emotions. In that case, self-regulation facilitates the process of redirection upon facing an obstacle and, more importantly, the development of a more effective response the next time. In other words, people who are able to regulate their emotions are likely to increase their self-awareness regarding their style and use of perseverance, which enables them to navigate through difficult obstacles and challenging setbacks.

For the purposes of this discussion, I define *emotionally intelligent perseverance* as "the ability to use emotional stability and self-regulation to identify, come to terms with, and redirect from obstacles to the achievement of short- and long-term goals in all domains of life, which produces a form of perseverance that is both sustainable and satisfying in its own right."

The following section provides an assessment of Duckworth's extant measures of perseverance and some novel questions that you can use to assess your current emotional state with perseverance. Finally, this chapter concludes with recommendations for how to cultivate emotionally intelligent perseverance in both self and others.

My Experience with Perseverance

My experience with perseverance has been a key element of my life, particularly as it relates to overcoming obstacles and carrying on in the face of extreme setbacks. As discussed in chapter 3, several key periods of my life required perseverance. This key ingredient to life meant that I needed the right amount of emotion to persevere through life's challenges. Emotion and persistence helped me through all my academic pursuits. For example, when I first decided to complete my university degree, I identified learning gaps that would be challenging

---

[182] Duckworth, *Grit*; Duckworth et al., "Grit."

obstacles. I had to relearn and acquire academic skills not developed during secondary education in a short time frame. To cope with these issues and avoid the feelings of inadequacy that had long plagued me, I had to develop a growth mindset. This change from a fixed to a growth mindset represented an essential change in my cognitive attitude to life. Failure was no longer a fixed condition to my success; instead, it was flexible as long as I showed up and worked hard daily. It helped me foster a belief that sustained effort over time would improve my skills. One tool I used to advance this mindset was deliberate practice. Reading and rereading texts as many times as I needed daily and for many hours helped me achieve my academic goals. It also helped me advance my studies toward my career.

My perspective on perseverance changed from adolescence to adulthood, and it continues to evolve into something that requires more grit. I used to think that a small amount of effort was needed to complete a menial task. I always treated perseverance as a race that would end as quickly as it started. During my financial career, I exhibited perseverance while working long hours to achieve my targets, motivated primarily by career advancement and financial gain. While the work I undertook during this period of my life constituted perseverance, I would not describe that period of my life as being as much characterized by *emotionally intelligent* perseverance. My career required me to develop and perform with more sophistication. Thus, I needed a new approach that would improve my stamina. Running a short race is different from running a marathon. The latter requires a sophisticated training approach that can build more resilience with more sustained effort.

Elsewhere in this chapter and book, I discuss the possible experience of viewing obstacles as a challenge rather than an insurmountable setback. If we view obstacles as challenges, it helps us to aspire to loftier goals. The goal is to implement the right emotional intelligence tools in our lives to find more enjoyment while minimizing suffering as we power through obstacles. Of course, this was patently *not* my experience of persevering through the Great Recession and its consequences. In saying that, I don't expect you to relish the vast and devastating setbacks in your life. Instead, try to change your perspective on the day-to-day challenges you experience. Then when you accomplish a goal, you will feel that achieving them can outweigh the annoyance associated with any of the obstacles that have arisen in the first place. In the instance of my existential crisis and rebirth, I had to use every tool at my disposal. These tools helped me redirect my effort to persevere toward the goal of a new career in teaching and psychology.

Passion and persistence were essential to grit, and so was nurturing emotional knowledge to build more stability in my personality. Learning how to self-regulate my behavior proved to be an asset when driven to performance rather than idleness throughout my doctoral process. Constantly cultivating these constructs led to less impulsive behavior, thanks in part to my ability to self-regulate. These enhanced abilities enabled me to move forward even when the writing process felt impossible. Eventually, I learned how to succeed in earning my degree. My past experiences helped me realize that, even in the face of immense difficulty, I did possess the skills I needed to refuse to give up; however, I stopped viewing perseverance as an innate skill that was needed sometimes but ended when the obstacle was removed from my path. Instead, I worked hard to understand perseverance in both the daily tasks and the seemingly insurmountable ones and cultivated a mindset that enabled me to view obstacles as a fact of life, but one that I would be able to circumvent through grit.

Measures/Outcomes

In this section of the chapter, I first provide the items from Duckworth's grit scale related to perseverance, which will enable you to determine a baseline for your grit-related level of perseverance. Then I encourage self-reflection and expansion of the concept by providing questions that will enable you to assess the degree to which you practice emotionally intelligent perseverance. Finally, I provide several (while many other and individualized positive outcomes are possible) potential outcomes that can occur upon cultivating and practicing this skill.

Grit-Scale Perseverance Measures

Duckworth's grit scale asked individuals to rate themselves on a scale from a 1 (not like me at all) to a 5 (very much like me). The even-numbered questions are those related specifically to perseverance.

2. Setbacks don't discourage me. I don't give up easily.
4. I am a hard worker.
6. I finish whatever I begin.
8. I am diligent. I never give up.
10. I have overcome setbacks to conquer an important challenge.

To determine your score on only the perseverance measures of Duckworth's grit scale, add your scores for each of these questions and divide by 5, to yield a maximum score of 5 and a minimum score of 1. While this instrument can serve as a reliable baseline to measure how gritty and perseverant you are for achievement, please remember that your perseverance improves with practice. Thus, it is possible to become more perseverant and enjoy the results of your perseverance more in each domain of life with emotional intelligence tools. These ideas appear in the final section of this chapter.

Measuring Emotionally Intelligent Perseverance

Before moving to a set of strategies for expanding your emotionally intelligent perseverance, it is important to practice the skills of self-reflection to consider your baseline in terms of perseverance in general and how you experience your perseverance. As with those in the previous chapter, the aim of providing these questions is not to formalize a scale for defining emotionally intelligent perseverance. As an alternative, it offers a template of questions that will enable you to consider your current experience and understanding of the concept before building on it in more detail. The first set of questions can help you assess the general sense with which you relate to the concepts of perseverance and resilience in terms of overall experience and identity.

1. Do you understand your perseverance as part of your identity or take pride in your perseverant actions?
2. Do you experience satisfaction as a result of overcoming obstacles?
3. Do you engage in a day-to-day process of building and maintaining resiliency?

To measure the element of satisfaction in relation to the *continual* performance of perseverance rather than its outcomes, the questions presented here relate more to your feelings and responses to overcoming obstacles rather than your overall ability to do so.

4. Do you feel a sense of pride when you redirect yourself from inaction to action by regulating emotions of defeat or tending to symptoms of burnout?
5. When you think or talk about a successful outcome you achieved, do you consider only the end result, or do you also credit the importance of the trials and difficulties you overcame on the way there?
6. Do you celebrate small achievements and short-term goals, or do you wait to celebrate until an entire task or aim has been accomplished?

Finally, the following questions are related to helping other individuals develop and maintain their emotionally intelligent perseverance:

7. Are you able to recognize perseverance and identify obstacles to persistence in other individuals (students, children, and employees, for example)?
8. Do you encourage others to identify and celebrate their moments of resilience and perseverance, both large and small?

Before moving to practical suggestions associated with developing an emotionally intelligent form of perseverance, the following sections address potential outcomes related to doing so.

The More Satisfaction You Take in Overcoming Obstacles, the Less Daunting They Seem

By cultivating your enjoyment of and sense of pride in overcoming obstacles, you are likely to notice an important shift in how you approach such challenges in the first place. It is worth noting there that Nietzsche proposed suffering to be an integral part of the human condition, which enables individuals to strive for greatness. As discussed in chapter 2, Nietzsche suggested that a life void of suffering was a life not lived because the journey through suffering yields the extensive satisfaction of overcoming obstacles.

> The discipline of suffering, of great suffering—do you not know that only this discipline has created all enhancements of man so far? That tension of the soul in unhappiness which cultivates its strength, its shudders face to face with great ruin, its inventiveness and courage in enduring, preserving, interpreting, and exploiting suffering, and whatever has been granted to it of profundity, secret, mask, spirit, cunning, greatness—was it not granted to it through suffering, through the discipline of great suffering?[183]

---

[183] Friedrich Nietzsche, *Basic Writings of Nietzsche* (New York: Modern Library, 2009), 344.

This practice is, in part, because the continual practice of overcoming obstacles and making strides in all aspects of life reinforces your view that you will be able to do so. More than that though, taking pride and pleasure in each action—large and small—that demonstrates your perseverance means that you will begin to anticipate that sensation upon first identifying an obstacle. When you cultivate and choose to focus on your future feeling of enjoyment after surpassing a challenge rather than the challenge itself, it will provide you with the strength to harness that feeling. Thereby overcoming obstacles with more and more emotionally intelligent perseverance is the result. This point is not to minimize the challenges you may face or suggest that perseverance will not require hard and painful work. However, shifting the timeline of your focus from the hard work itself to its anticipated positive short-term outcomes can provide an additional reserve of strength. More importantly, practicing this type of perseverance means that you do not need to rely on the long-term, far-off achievement to serve as the motivating factor but can take pride and pleasure in the incremental achievements you make along the way.

Expanded Definition = Expanded Domains

The type of emotionally intelligent perseverance addressed in this chapter can be applied to all domains of life. At the same time, this may seem obvious (in that, of course, perseverance is necessary for parenting or marriage or pursuing hobbies, as well as for work), the positive applications of a reframed understanding of emotionally intelligent perseverance may be less apparent. For example, while taking pride in meeting and overcoming work challenges is a frequently articulated concept ("I enjoy my career because it presents new challenges every day"), we are less likely to apply this mindset to other domains of life ("I enjoy and take pride in the process of identifying and working through a problem with my spouse"). While most individuals would prefer those relational and more leisure-driven aspects of life devoid of challenges, it is not feasible. This avoidance to avoid challenges is normal, but people complicate the process because of the norms and mores of society's values. However, emotionally intelligent perseverance offers an opportunity to derive satisfaction from continually meeting challenges in specific areas of life. This change in our approach causes us to have positive connotations of "obstacles" while driving for realistic results.

Expanding Emotionally Intelligent Perseverance
Celebrate Small Achievements

One essential tool to grow your emotionally intelligent perseverance is to celebrate small achievements and effective redirections. This practice dovetails with that of effective goal setting as well, as it is important to develop cohesive short- as well as long-term goals. Be sure to implement a practice of celebrating small achievements in a way that works for you. What you expect will facilitate your ongoing perseverance. This understanding should be tailored to your preferences and should include the identification of frequent, measurable milestones. Similarly, be sure to help your children, students, or employees implement small celebrations of small milestones in order to reinforce perseverant behaviors.

Likewise, be sure to celebrate positive redirections or experiences of overcoming obstacles. After an unexpected challenge slows your progress, celebrate the positive aspects of how you dealt with it, learn from the negative ones, and focus on the positives of being back on track. Try to avoid idle thinking and dwelling on the negative time during which you were not productive. This practice is very closely related to the importance of positive self-talk. This positive approach enables you to action and away from sentiments that paralyze your thinking and behavior.

For the reasons previously mentioned, we should avoid damaging self-talk, so be kind when talking about yourself. Some examples of destructive self-talk include "I'm a failure for having become distracted" or "This obstacle is insurmountable for me." Self-talk is not productive, and it will paralyze you from moving forward in your life. As a replacement, say things more along the lines of "I worked hard to recognize and to present a workable solution to that obstacle." This change in language helps you reframe negativity to one of pride for having overcome any problem. It can make a significant difference in achievement and satisfaction outcomes in life. Positive self-talk and a favorable attitude can change your thinking. Don't fall into the trap as a victim; instead, think about the options to help you solve the problem. Remember that failure is not a permanent condition that you should avoid but an opportunity to grow your grit and emotional intelligence to improve your satisfaction in life. When you feel stuck on a task or in life, then change a variable and watch how your perspective and life changes.

Similarly, affirmative language can help you instill emotionally intelligent perseverance in others. Be sure to redirect language if you hear others performing behaviors counter to emotionally intelligent perseverance. For example, it would be best to focus only on significant and long-term goals while ignoring the small ones. This focus matters because we should not dwell on the negative outcomes of an obstacle or challenge rather than celebrate having overcome it. Neglecting to recognize issues can affect perseverance and affirm and augment positive perseverant behaviors.

Grow Your Growth Mindset

Further, developing your growth mindset can be an important tool to improve your emotionally intelligent perseverance. Again, this recommendation is closely correlated with self-talk and language that prioritizes ability to grow, develop new skills, and overcome new obstacles rather than considering challenges—and our ability to cope with them—permanently fixed. In terms of parenting applications, an important shift in relation to the growth mindset is a transition from language like "You're so talented at that" to affirmations more in the vein of "I'm proud of the way you worked hard to get better at that."

Through its close association with resilience, perseverance is key to life satisfaction. It facilitates individuals' ability to move past challenges. By adding elements of emotional intelligence to this practice—specifically identifying, managing, and redirecting emotions through the tools of emotional stability and self-regulation—it is possible to learn to derive satisfaction and pride from your responses to such challenges rather than delighting only in end results. As demonstrated in this chapter's outcome and recommendations sections, emotionally intelligent perseverance can serve you in diverse domains of life, including vocational, hobby-related, parenting, and relational interactions. In the next chapter, we will shift our focus to the importance of consistency and how you can use emotional intelligence tools to ensure that your work in developing more emotionally intelligent passion and perseverance is sustainable over time.

CHAPTER 8

Consistency

Before moving to a conclusion, my purpose in this chapter is to address the element that will help you sustain your emotionally intelligent passion and emotionally intelligent perseverance and propel this growth into the future: consistency. While moments of passion and examples of perseverance are worth celebrating, what makes these concepts unique in the context of grit and emotional intelligence is their longevity. Consistency of both passion and perseverance is what facilitates the accomplishment of *long-term* goals. Passion requires consistency of interest, or it will fade; likewise, goal accomplishment requires consistently applied perseverance. While a burst of passion— or the act of persevering in the face of a single or several obstacles— can result in the accomplishment of a short-term aim, both concepts require consistent application if they are to yield the accomplishment of many long-term goals and, thereby, to drive a practical approach to life satisfaction.

In this chapter, I address two concepts related to consistency: conscientiousness and self-control. I explain how both concepts relate to the tools of emotional intelligence and identify several of their applications to long-term goals in all domains of life. I then provide several questions that can be used to assess and measure consistency and propose potential outcomes associated with the application of consistency. Finally, I provide practical suggestions for ways to grow sustainable consistency.

Conscientiousness

Like perseverance, the notion of conscientiousness is more frequently addressed to grit and consequently with work domains than life satisfaction and more relational aspects of life. Conscientiousness is one of the traits in the "Big Five" model of personality alongside extraversion, agreeableness, neuroticism, and openness. "The tendency to be organized, responsible, and hardworking" requires elevated levels of conscientiousness (*APA Dictionary of Psychology*). In addition, several studies have identified conscientiousness as a personality trait that overlaps with grit to predict success, including military, academic achievement, and work-based settings.[184]

Importantly, however, conscientiousness also has less obvious associations with life satisfaction and nonwork domains. While hard work, responsibility, and organization are necessary for accomplishing vocational goals, they also facilitate fulfillment through several key mechanisms. First, conscientiousness is understood as one end of a spectrum, the other side of which is lack of direction. Conscientiousness then has an orientating function that can be applied to all domains of life. Consistent application of hard work, organization, and responsibility prevent directionlessness in relationships, passion projects, parenting, and other domains, in addition to its role in work-based success.

---

[184] Duckworth, *Grit*; Dweck, *Mindset*; Eskreis Winkler et al., "Using Wise Interventions"; Dennis R. Kelly, Michael D. Matthews, and Paul T. Bartone, "Grit and Hardiness as Predictors of Performance among West Point Cadets," *Military Psychology* 26, no. 4 (2017; 2014): 327–342.

Therefore, conscientiousness has a key relationship to life satisfaction by providing direction.

Further, conscientiousness is a key driver of longevity. For example, researchers have found that conscientiousness enables people to remain focused and disciplined, especially in executing complex tasks that demand focused mental volition.[185] Similarly, individuals who are both gritty and exhibit high levels of conscientiousness are more likely to manifest higher levels of stamina.[186] This finding is crucial since it is necessary to persevere through complex challenges while pursuing long-term goals with consistent levels of interest and purpose.

Consistency has also been shown to be a better predictor of marriage outcomes than grit, particularly when applied alongside other personality traits. For example, emotional stability, agreeableness, and conscientiousness were significant predictors of marriage interval than grit.[187] In addition, while grit is a predictor of marriage length only among men, conscientiousness is a significant predictor of marriage longevity for both men and women. One potential reason for the role of conscientiousness and marriage longevity is its close connection with emotional intelligence. The practice of conscientiousness requires self-regulation of emotional input and output, which is a key aspect of emotional intelligence.[188]

In a neurological sense too, it is fitting that conscientiousness would be linked to aspects of emotional intelligence. The brain's prefrontal cortex is specialized for cognitive functioning, including self-regulating behavior, emotional regulation, impulse control, and cognitive control

---

[185] Abuhassan and Bates, "Grit Distinguishing."
[186] Angela L. Duckworth and James J. Gross, "Self-Control and Grit: Related but Separable Determinants of Success," *Current Directions in Psychological Science: A Journal of the American Psychological Society* 23, no. 5 (2014): 319–325.
[187] Brent W. Roberts et al., "The Power of Personality: The Comparative Validity of Personality Traits, Socioeconomic Status, and Cognitive Ability for Predicting Important Life Outcomes," *Perspectives on Psychological Science* 2, no. 4 (2007): 313–345.
[188] Libbrecht et al., "Emotional Intelligence."

for processing information.[189] Thus, researchers linked subregions of the prefrontal cortex to behaviors associated with conscientiousness. They found that lesions to this area disrupted the individuals' ability to plan activities, set goals, complete activities, and understand the complexity of social interactions.

Self-Control

Similarly, the concept of self-control is closely related to consistency and preference for long-term over short-term aims. The *APA Dictionary of Psychology* defines the term as

> the ability to be in command of one's behavior (overt, covert, emotional, or physical) and to restrain or inhibit one's impulses. In circumstances in which short-term gain is pitted against long-term greater gain, self-control is the ability to opt for the long-term outcome.

This definition fits in the context of this study on the interaction between grit and emotional intelligence in producing life satisfaction. In addition, it emphasizes self-regulation and the importance of consciously selecting a long- rather than a short-term outcome.

Self-control is often categorized alongside traits including deliberate practice and growth mindset, as addressed throughout this treatise. Importantly, self-control is closely connected to the concept of time management. Indeed, many of the practical applications of opting for the long-term outcome are related to temporal choices. For example, self-control is an essential characteristic in understanding people's ability to use their time more purposefully. Duckworth identified certain behaviors that grit paragons use to avoid wasting time: turning

---

[189] Song Wang et al., "Grit and the Brain: Spontaneous Activity of the Dorsomedial Prefrontal Cortex Mediates the Relationship between the Trait Grit and Academic Performance," *Social Cognitive and Affective Neuroscience* 12, no. 3 (2017): 452–460.

off the mobile device, avoiding toggling back and forth from one task to another, and removing the impulse to text when engaged in a task that requires a high degree of mental volition.[190]

My Experience with Consistency

While many phases of my life required conscientiousness and self-control to power the tools of grit, I have, over time, been able to cultivate those skills in order to maintain interest continually; frequently overcome obstacles; and repeatedly continue in the pursuit of whatever vocational, relational, or academic goal I have set. An early example of my use of emotionally intelligent consistency was how I viewed my loneliness as a sanctuary during my childhood. As a result, I lacked sufficient opportunities to experience an engaging learning environment and interact with other students. Almost like a repeated mantra in my thoughts about the value of my own thinking and mind helped me consistently reset my mindset and reframe my thoughts.

During my undergraduate education, I exhibited consistency by rereading my course texts. However, other students did not need to employ this level of daily consistency. This daily discipline meant quite literally that I was "showing up" again and again by repeatedly reading to understand the same piece of writing. This tool helped me achieve my aim of graduating with my undergraduate degree while beginning the long process of cultivating my self-control and conscientiousness. This effort moved me toward pursuing *sustainable*, emotionally intelligent passion and emotionally intelligent perseverance.

Now we return to the dissertation writing example. The dedication needed to complete my manuscript was not easy to come by. The passion, perseverance, and consistency required a great deal of inner strength to power me to the finish line. As mentioned in the previous sections, I needed to sustain my interest, purpose, and passion over time and persevere through obstacles that I faced. More than that

---

[190] Duckworth, *Grit*.

though, I needed to use those tools repeatedly to continue to move forward in the process. I felt like I suffered greatly through this creative process, but I could channel this frustration to power through some difficult times. The consistency I employed enabled me to power the grit tools and make them work for me. It also helped me achieve my goals.

Working several jobs consistently during this process wasn't easy. Trying to maintain my interest in the project that caused me much suffering was hard. However, it was important to show up day after day to progress toward my goals. I never really realized how much pressure needed to build to mobilize into action to maintain the consistency necessary to persevere through significant hardships. I remember being emotional partly because I felt the manuscript's creation was breaking me. These emotions were more potent by the time constraints that I faced working several jobs. Trying to find the time to write daily was hard, and it was even harder to have less free time to relax.

In this situation, my process required self-regulation and accepting, then addressing my emotions in order to find the strength to move forward again and again. And again, the fact that, as I progressed throughout my degree and conducted my study, I also came to understand the importance of consistency. Its role in powering my progress was beneficial. Unlike my colleagues who were undertaking degrees in different fields, I learned to adjust my thoughts and behaviors, as readers of this book now know. Rather than a vague sense that I needed to make adjustments to move forward, I had the understanding and knowledge to back this up and motivate myself to progress despite the struggle and difficulty. It couldn't be more evident to me that consistency, passion, and perseverance were imperative to me as I attempted to achieve my goal. It goes beyond achievement too, because I needed this consistency in order to feel a sense of accomplishment, distinction, and satisfaction.

Measures and Outcomes

As addressed in the previous two chapters, the first step in cultivating the type of consistency that can yield life satisfaction is through the tools of self-awareness and self-evaluation. The following sets of questions are meant to prompt reflection on your current level of and areas of improvement for consistency, broken down into consistency of passion, consistency of perseverance, and inspiring consistency in others.

Consistent Passion

Consistency of passion requires maintaining a consistent awareness of interest and purpose. As mentioned about conscientiousness, this type of consistency has key applications in relationships and other domains of life. Use the following questions to assess your current degree of consistency concerning passion:

1. Do new interests frequently supplant your old ones, or do they tend to remain stable across time?
2. Do you frequently or infrequently lose interest in things that are important to your spouse/partner/children/students but not necessarily to you? If so, do you have tools to recreate this interest and engage with it over time?
3. Do you find that you work harder, with more organization, and more responsibly on tasks when your interest and purpose levels are high? What do you do when these are low?
4. What reminders, if any, do you use with the broader and longer-term purpose of your vocational, relational, hobby, academic, or other personal goals?

While the answers to these questions are highly individualized, they should stimulate thinking about subjective experiences regardless of the person answering them. If we become self-aware, then we are ready to regulate our behavior. As a result, the behavioral possibilities are boundless with endless potential to grow into the person we want.

Consistent Perseverance

While perseverance and consistency are closely related, it is important to develop an awareness of the consistency or inconsistency with which you practice emotionally intelligent perseverance. Long-term persistence, of the type that can improve life satisfaction, is made up of a continual series of perseverant acts. These acts, if implemented correctly, become habitual. The following questions focus on helping you evaluate the consistency and deliberateness with which you practice perseverance:

1. Do you have any constructive behaviors related to overcoming obstacles that you would consider purposeful or habitual?
2. Would you consider yourself self-controlled or impulsive in relation to the process of working toward short- and long-term goals?
3. Would you consider yourself self-controlled or impulsive in relation to time management?
4. Do you experience a feeling of directionlessness when obstacles arise?

Importantly, these questions are not necessarily about the notions of pride and enjoyment to overcome obstacles, as mentioned in the previous chapter. Instead, these items are related to the characteristics of conscientiousness and self-control that build habitual behaviors like writing.

Encouraging Consistency in Others

While your own consistency is key in a relational sense, it is also important that any work you do to encourage those around you—particularly children, students, and employees—to practice emotionally intelligent passion and perseverance also encourages consistency in these areas. The purpose of the following questions is to prompt considerations of how you model consistency for others and how you encourage consistency in others.

1. Do you tend to have unspoken expectations of others that do not agree with expressions of gratitude, praise, acknowledgment, respect, congratulations, etc.? Or do you tend to express a positive reaction each time an event occurs, only the first time, or not at all?
2. Do you model strategies associated with maintaining consistent passion (interest and purpose) for others?
3. Do you model strategies associated with maintaining consistent perseverance (self-control and time management, for example) for others?

Although these questions only function as a starting point, they should help you conduct a preliminary assessment in terms of your current consistency applications. The key outcome associated with improved consistency is the creation of sustainable habits.

Consistency Creates Sustainable Habits

The most important outcome, even side effect, of consistency is that it facilitates the creation of habits. For example, when a behavior associated with maintaining emotionally intelligent passion or perseverance becomes habitual, it mitigates the time required to analyze the problem. Then implement a strategy for getting back on track and repeat the process. Instead, you begin to use the habitual tool without needing to use as much thought, motivation, or effort to do so. While this does not mean that your strategies for time management, self-control, organization, responsibility, diligence, interest, purpose, and overcoming obstacles will be simple or easy, it does mean that you will be more likely to turn to them quickly and efficiently. In all the strategies addressed in the next section then, consider ways in which you can perform key behaviors consistently enough and for long enough (twenty-one days in a row of consistent practice tends to be the agreed-upon length of time after which a habit is created) to make them second nature.

Sustainable Consistency

Concerning the recommendations addressed in the previous chapters, consider and implement ways in which you can become more consistent with your performance of strategies and proliferation of key attitudes. About passion, consider the consistent use of a deliberate practice journal and consistent ways in which you can blend effort with play in both your own tasks and those of others. About perseverance, evaluate and improve the consistency with which you celebrate small achievements and encourage the growth mindset. Finally, concerning the elements of conscientiousness and self-control addressed in this chapter, the following sections provide practical recommendations for sustainable consistency.

Time Management

Practices of effective time management can help maintain consistent passion and ameliorate obstacles to consistent perseverance. When you manage time efficiently, you also develop habits related to effective time management. Thus, you feed your passion, which develops perseverance to achieve their full potential in terms of outcomes. Furthermore, the idea that emotional intelligence being an important element to time management means you can promote life satisfaction in various aspects of life, such as work or academic-type tasks and relational and leadership-based tasks.

A key aspect of time management, for example, is identifying the time of day and settings during which you are most effective and scheduling your most difficult tasks for that time. A frequently cited example of this common strategy is the following: If you're at optimum functionality early morning, schedule your most creative or difficult work task for the morning. Try to refrain from checking and answering straightforward emails until a time of day when your productivity is lower. However, a key application of this paradigm shift in how we think about grit and emotional intelligence is the applicability of strategies like this to relational domains as well. For example, one application of emotionally intelligent passion is participating in and engaging with the interests of a spouse or partner. This point is essential because their interests don't always align perfectly with your own. Yet we find ourselves engaged in their interests. While romantic and other interpersonal relationships are not scheduled to the same extent as is work, that does not mean that time management should be absent from your relations with others. Another example is if your partner's primary passion is something for which you have little concern, but you are working to engage more with their interests, consider the time at which you have the energy for such conversations, and choose those times to ask open-ended questions about their passion. This show of interest can work similarly in various aspects of parenting, coaching, teaching, and leading.

Showing up for the Banal as Well as the Watershed Moments

Another key expression of emotionally intelligent consistency is bringing energy, effective strategies, and functional habits to small and key moments. Habits are unlikely to be formed if they are only used when needed most. It is unlikely to form a habit when drastic, pivotal moments emerge, such as a significant marital conflict, a key parenting dilemma, or a major work task obstacle. While these areas are essential for such skills as self-awareness, self-regulation, passion, and perseverance, it is likewise imperative to show up daily for all eventualities. For instance, banal spousal interactions, daily parenting challenges, and drafting an email response to an employee might appear as small and even inconsequential.

On the other hand, they have the potential to improve the lives of those you are interacting with, which in turn improves your life satisfaction. If we do little things today, they have the potential to build something more extraordinary and unforeseen tomorrow. In this way, you can enable effective strategies to become habits that propel you toward life satisfaction.

CONCLUSION

A paradigm shift from achievement to life satisfaction—using the concepts of grit and emotional intelligence—is necessary on both an individual and a psychological field level. Based on a novel study of grit, emotional intelligence, age, and gender, I found that grit and emotional intelligence both have some degree of influence on life satisfaction. This book expands and builds on those findings and puts them into terms that facilitate their logical conclusions in terms of practical applications. Part 1 of this book provided introductory material and a concise report of my study, including definitions and the gap in previous literature, a literature review of relevant extant research on the subject, my story, methodological considerations, and results.

Part 2 of this book moved toward the practical considerations regarding how to grow and apply emotionally intelligent grit practices of passion, perseverance, and consistency. Chapter 5 addressed research and recommendations on why grit and emotional intelligence are both learnable, rather than innate, skills. It discussed the idea of social learning theory, growth mindset, deliberate practice, and the development of emotional intelligence before providing self-reflection questions to enable you to assess the degree to which you were approaching the concepts from a fixed or growth mindset and to reflect on how to change your perspective on the learnability of these competencies to ensure your success in the remainder of this book.

In chapter 6, I addressed the concept of emotionally intelligent passion and invited a shift in conceptualizing the term from its connotation of relating to heated, torrid, and transitory emotions to a more staid, solid, and long-term type of devotion. I addressed the psychological concept of passion as researchers have defined it across time before defining *emotionally intelligent passion* as self-aware, strong, and sustainable dedication. People can channel emotionally intelligent passion through self-regulation, motivation, and practice, which can be cultivated in others' empathy. I also addressed the fact that passion can be present in both work and nonwork domains and surveyed extant literature on the concept of practice and pleasure. I clarified the overlap between the concepts of passion and self-improvement then proposed several questions for measuring emotionally intelligent passion. In terms of passion's outcomes, I identified the shift from interest to purpose, the sustainment of effort, and the creation of more passion as possible results of cultivating emotionally intelligent passion. Finally, I suggested using a deliberate practice journal and blending effort with play as a means of growing emotionally intelligent passion.

In chapters 7 and 8, I addressed the concept of emotionally intelligent perseverance (the ability to use emotional stability and self-regulation to identify, come to terms with, and redirect from obstacles to the achievement of short- and long-term goals in all domains of life, which produces a form of perseverance that is both sustainable and satisfying in its own right) in relation to the concept of resilience, including how both relate to the concept of hardiness and the growth mindset. I also considered the role of emotional stability and self-regulation concerning the capacity to overcome obstacles required for sustainable perseverance. After presenting questions for the self-assessment of emotionally intelligent perseverance, I suggested its capacity to help you begin to take more satisfaction in overcoming obstacles and its applicability to various domains of life. To expand emotionally intelligent perseverance, I recommended celebrating small achievements and growing the growth mindset.

I defined emotionally intelligent consistency as "the engine that powers emotionally intelligent passion and emotionally intelligent perseverance." This definition places importance on the day-to-day act of "showing up," which leads to repeated acts of emotionally intelligent passion and perseverance. I first addressed the relationship of consistency to conscientiousness and self-control before providing measures for self-reflection concerning consistent passion and consistent perseverance and encouraging consistency in others. Next, I proposed that the potential outcome of emotionally intelligent consistency is the creation of sustainable habits and suggested that this can be accomplished via time management and showing up for the banal as well as the watershed moments. Before we move to a conclusion with final recommendations for creating, growing, and maintaining your practice of emotionally intelligent grit to achieve life satisfaction, it is important to highlight some of the study's practical implications.

Implications for Practice

First, there are several important practical implications related to the practice of grit and emotional intelligence. One of the key implications of the fact that both skills are learnable rather than innate is that educators and education administrators should de-emphasize "talent" and intelligence measures and should implement more tools and curricula that facilitate the development of these concepts. For example, suppose you've read this book as a parent, caregiver, or educator. In that case, you can use the tools you've learned to help individual children succeed in developing this skill. However, it should be emphasized on a broader policy and curricular level. This proposed change could have significant implications for those who are taught at an early age the principles of perseverance and passion associated with grit, alongside the competencies associated with emotional intelligence.

Emotional intelligence can also have important and widespread practical applications given its important relationship to life satisfaction. If the concept is given more credence in schools and workplaces, more individuals would have the time and tools necessary for its cultivation. This policy change could lead to more prevalent life satisfaction among larger proportions of the population. Put more strongly, societies interested in reducing suicide and mortality rates should develop and implement etiology programs that build sustainable satisfaction throughout an individual's life through emotional intelligence programs.

This process should start early in primary education to teach children the principles and mechanisms associated with emotional and life satisfaction, including programs for improving grit, self-esteem, emotional intelligence, and life satisfaction. This practical implication for education extends to adult managerial roles as well. Supervisors who influence subordinates, teachers who influence students, and parents who influence children might examine new ways to improve and develop better behaviors that could influence the degree of grit and emotional intelligence to yield widespread increases in life satisfaction.

Recommendations for Personal Implementation

As you move forward in applying the recommendations proposed in this book into various domains of your life, I'd recommend returning as often as necessary to the reflective questions throughout this book. Not only will these enable you to check in as you work to apply emotionally intelligent passion, perseverance, and consistency throughout your life, but they will also help you hone the self-assessment and self-regulation aspects of your emotional intelligence. Most centrally, be sure to remember that emotionally intelligent grit is learned, that you can build this skill over time and apply it to diverse domains of your life, and that—as these skills grow—the process of implementing them becomes increasingly efficacious and indeed pleasurable.

I also recommend working on these applications in stages, both in terms of individual concepts and in terms of the areas of life to which they apply. Because this book is based most centrally on a paradigm shift from achievement to life satisfaction, its goal is a long-term and sustainable outcome rather than a flash in the pan. Suppose you implement its recommendations gradually and power them with emotionally intelligent passion, perseverance, and consistency. In that case, you may find that it has a sustainable snowball effect: compounding improvements in your satisfaction with various areas of life.

As the final point of departure, I ask you to embrace failure rather than run from it. That way, you search diligently for a solution to the problem. Then you can push forward in a noble direction. Be open to new experiences that provide you with a productive and profitable outcome. Remember to change a variable when life doesn't appear fulfilling while trusting the process to live a life worth living. I've now completed an interpretation of the events and manifold variables responsible for influencing life satisfaction.

BIBLIOGRAPHY

Abuhassan, Abedrahman and Timothy C. Bates. "Grit Distinguishing Effortful Persistence from Conscientiousness." *Journal of Individual Differences* 36, no. 4 (2015): 205–214.

Ackley, Dana. "Emotional Intelligence: A Practical Review of Models, Measures, and Applications." *Consulting Psychology Journal* 68, no. 4 (2016): 269–286.

Allis, Pam and Michael O'Driscoll. "Positive Effects of Nonwork-to-Work Facilitation on Well-being in Work, Family and Personal Domains." *Journal of Managerial Psychology* 23, no. 3 (2008): 273–291.

American Psychiatric Association. *Diagnostic and Statistical Manual of Mental Disorders: DSM-5.* Arlington, VA: American Psychiatric Association, 2013.

Anderson, John. "'Operation Varsity Blues: The College Admissions Scandal' Review: Dishonor System." *Wall Street Journal*, March 16, 2021. https://www.wsj.com/articles/operation-varsity-blues-the-college-admissions-scandal-review-dishonor-system-11615930560.

Antaramian, Susan. "The Importance of Very High Life Satisfaction for Students' Academic Success." *Cogent Education* 4, no. 1 (2017).

Anthes, Emily." The Glossary of Happiness," *The New Yorker*. May 12, 2016, https://www.newyorker.com/tech/annals-of-technology/the-glossary-of-happiness.

Aurelius, Marcus, Martin Hammond, and Diskin Clay. *Meditations*. New York: Penguin Classics, 2006.

Bandura, Albert. "Self-Efficacy: Toward a Unifying Theory of Behavioral Change." *Psychological Review* 84, no. 2 (1977): 191–215. https://doi.org/10.1037/0033-295X.84.2.191.

Bar-On, Reuven. *Technical Manual for the Emotional Quotient Inventory*. Toronto: Multi-Health Systems, 1997.

Barr, Donald A. "Science as Superstition: Selecting Medical Students." *The Lancet* 376, no. 9742 (2010): 678–679.

Bennett, Jeff, and Eric Morath, "U.S. Remaining Stake in General Motors." *Wall Street Journal*, December 9, 2013, https://www.wsj.com/articles/SB10001424052748704362004575000841720318942.

Beutel, Manfred E., Heide Glaesmer, Jörg Wiltink, Hanna Marian, and Elmar Brähler. "Life Satisfaction, Anxiety, Depression and Resilience across the Life Span of Men." *The Aging Male* 13, no. 1 (2010): 32–39.

Biden, Joe. "President Joe Biden Delivers His First State of the Union Address." CNBC, 28 April 2021. https://www.youtube.com/watch?v=dggKaPXt0gI.

Brown, Ralph. "Building Children and Young people's Resilience: Lessons from Psychology." *International Journal of Disaster Risk Reduction* 14 (2015): 115–124.

Bass, Bernard M., and Ronald E. Riggio, *Transformational Leadership*, 2nd ed. Mahwah, N.J: L. Erlbaum Associates, 2006.

Cabello, Rosario, Miguel A. Sorrel, Irene Fernández-Pinto, Natalio Extremera, and Pablo Fernández-Berrocal. "Age and Gender Differences in Ability Emotional Intelligence in Adults: A Cross-Sectional Study." *Developmental Psychology* 52, no. 9 (2016): 1486–1492.

Camus, Albert. *The Plague*. New York: Vintage, 1991. First Published 1947 by Gallimard.

Carney, John. "The Secret History of Glass-Steagall." *Wall Street Journal*, July 19, 2016. https://www.wsj.com/articles/BL-MBB-51646.

Ciarrochi, Joseph V., Amy Y. C. Chan, and Peter Caputi. "A Critical Evaluation of the Emotional Intelligence Construct." *Personality and Individual Differences* 28, no. 3 (2000): 539–561.

Conte, Jeffrey M. "A Review and Critique of Emotional Intelligence Measures." *Journal of Organizational Behavior* 26, no. 4 (2005): 433–440.

Corradini, Antonella and Alessandro Antonietti. "Mirror Neurons and Their Function in Cognitively Understood Empathy." *Consciousness and Cognition* 22, no. 3 (2013): 1152–1161.

Dambrun, Michaël and Matthieu Ricard. "Self-Centeredness and Selflessness: A Theory of Self-Based Psychological Functioning and Its Consequences for Happiness." *Review of General Psychology* 15, no. 2 (2011): 138–157.

David, Susan. "The Gift and Power of Emotional Courage." Filmed November 2017 in New Orleans, LA. TED video, 16:30. https://www.ted.com/talks/susan_david_the_gift_and_power_of_emotional_courage.

Davies, Kevin A., Andrew M. Lane, Tracey J. Devonport, and Jamie A. Scott. "Validity and Reliability of a Brief Emotional Intelligence

Scale (BEIS-10)." *Journal of Individual Differences* 31, no. 4 (2010): 198–208.

Deutschendorf, Harvey. "5 Ways Emotional Intelligence Can Boost Post-COVID-19 Workplace Communication." *FastCompany*, May 20, 2021, https://www.fastcompany.com/90638435/5-ways-emotional-intelligence-can-boost-post-covid-workplace-communication.

Dickens, Charles. *A Tale of Two Cities*. New York: Cosmopolitan Book Corporation, 1921. www.loc.gov/item/22004431/.

Diener, Ed, Samantha J. Heintzelman, Kostadin Kushlev, Louis Tay, Derrick Wirtz, Lesley D. Lutes, and Shigehiro Oishi. "Findings All Psychologists Should Know from the New Science on Subjective Well-being." *Canadian Psychology = Psychologie Canadienne* 58, no. 2 (2017): 87–104.

Driebusch, Corrie. "Lehman's Last Hires Look Back," *Wall Street Journal*, September 7, 2018. https://www.wsj.com/articles/lehmans-last-hires-look-back-1536321600.

Duckworth, Angela L. "Grit: The Power of Passion and Perseverance." Filmed 2013. TED Video, 6:01. https://www.ted.com/talks/angela_lee_duckworth_grit_the_power_of_passion_and_perseverance.

Duckworth, Angela. *Grit: The Power of Passion and Perseverance*. New York: Scribner, 2016.

Duckworth, Angela L., Christopher Peterson, Michael D. Matthews, and Dennis R. Kelly. "Grit: Perseverance and Passion for Long-Term Goals." *Journal of Personality and Social Psychology* 92, no. 6 (2007): 1087–1101.

Duckworth, Angela Lee and Patrick D. Quinn. "Development and Validation of the Short Grit Scale (Grit–S)." *Journal of Personality Assessment* 91, no. 2 (2009): 166–174.

Duckworth, Angela L., and Patrick D. Quinn. "Short Grit Scale." 2009, https://dx.doi.org/10.1037/t01598-000.

Duckworth, Angela Lee, Patrick D. Quinn, and Martin E. P. Seligman. "Positive Predictors of Teacher Effectiveness." *The Journal of Positive Psychology* 4, no. 6 (2009): 540–547.

Duckworth, Angela L., Patrick D. Quinn, Donald R. Lynam, Rolf Loeber, and Magda Stouthamer-Loeber. "Role of Test Motivation in Intelligence Testing." *Proceedings of the National Academy of Sciences* 108, no. 19 (2011): 7716–7720.

Duckworth, Angela and James J. Gross. "Self-Control and Grit: Related but Separable Determinants of Success." *Current Directions in Psychological Science: A Journal of the American Psychological Society* 23, no. 5 (2014): 319–325.

Duckworth, Angela L., David Weir, Eli Tsukayama, and David Kwok. "Who Does Well in Life? Conscientious Adults Excel in Both Objective and Subjective Success." *Frontiers in Psychology* 3, (2012): 356–363.

Dweck, Carol S. *Mindset: The New Psychology of Success*. New York: Random House, 2006.

Einstein, Albert. *Relativity: The Special and General Theory*, New York: Holt, 1921.

Ericsson, K. Anders and Neil Charness. "Expert Performance: Its Structure and Acquisition." *The American Psychologist* 49, no. 8 (1994): 725–747.

Eskreis-Winkler, Lauren, Elizabeth P. Shulman, Scott A. Beal, and Angela L. Duckworth. "The Grit Effect: Predicting Retention in the Military, the Workplace, School and Marriage." *Frontiers in Psychology* 5 (2014): 1–12.

Eskreis-Winkler, Lauren, Elizabeth P. Shulman, Victoria Young, Eli Tsukayama, Steven M. Brunwasser, and Angela L. Duckworth. "Using Wise Interventions to Motivate Deliberate Practice." *Journal of Personality and Social Psychology* 111, no. 5 (2016): 728–744.

Feist Gregory J., and Erica L. Rosenberg. *Psychology: Perspectives and Connections*. New York: McGraw-Hill, 2018.

Frankl, Victor. *Man's Search for Meaning*. Boston: Beacon Press, 2006.

Freud, Sigmund. *Beyond the Pleasure Principle*. Translated by C. J. M. Hubback. London, Vienna: International Psycho-Analytical, 1922. www.bartleby.com/276/.

Freud, Sigmund. *Civilization and Its Discontents*, 1930, trans. James Strachey. New York: Norton, 1961.

Froh, Jeffrey J., William J. Sefick, and Robert A. Emmons. "Counting Blessings in Early Adolescents: An Experimental Study of Gratitude and Subjective Well-being." *Journal of School Psychology* 46, no. 2 (2008): 213–233.

Gaffen, David, "The Bank of Goldman Sachs and Morgan Stanley?" *Wall Street Journal*, September 21, 2008. https://www.wsj.com/articles/BL-MB-4100.

Galbraith, John K. *The Economics of Innocent Fraud: Truth for Our Time*. Boston: Houghton Mifflin, 2004.

Galbraith, John K. *The Good Society: The Humane Agenda*. Boston: Houghton Mifflin, 1996.

Galbraith, John Kenneth. *The Great Crash, 1929*. Boston: Houghton Mifflin, 1955.

Galton, Francis. *Hereditary Genius: An Inquiry into Its Laws and Consequences*. London: Macmillan, 1892.

Ghule, Vishal and B. R. Shejwal. "The Role of Cognitive Hardiness in Health and Performance of Bank Managers." *Indian Journal of Health and Wellbeing* 7, no. 4 (2016): 383.

Gorgens-Ekermans, Gina and Chene Roux. "Revisiting the Emotional Intelligence and Transformational Leadership Debate: Does Emotional Intelligence Matter to Effective Leadership?" *SA Journal of Human Resource Management* 19, no. 2 (2021): e1–e13.

Gordon, Jon and Kathryn Gordon. *Relationship Grit: A True Story with Lessons to Stay Together, Grow Together, and Thrive Together*. Newark: John Wiley & Sons, 2020.

Grawitch, Matthew J., Patrick W. Maloney, Larissa K. Barber, and Stephanie E. Mooshegian. "Examining the Nomological Network of Satisfaction with Work-Life Balance." *Journal of Occupational Health Psychology* 18, no. 3 (2013): 276–284.

Guney, Sevgi, Temel Kalafat, and Murat Boysan. "Dimensions of Mental Health: Life Satisfaction, Anxiety and Depression: A Preventive Mental Health Study in Ankara University Students Population." *Procedia, Social and Behavioral Sciences* 2, no. 2 (2010): 1210–1213.

Guo, Jeff. "The Jobs That Really Smart People Avoid." *Washington Post*, January 12, 2017. https://www.washingtonpost.com/news/wonk/wp/2017/01/12/the-jobs-that-really-smart-people-avoid/.

Haimovitz, Kyla and Carol S. Dweck. "Parents' Views of Failure Predict Children's Fixed and Growth Intelligence Mind-Sets." *Psychological Science* 27, no. 6 (2016): 859–869.

Harms, P. D. and Marcus Credé. "Emotional Intelligence and Transformational and Transactional Leadership: A Meta-Analysis." *Journal of Leadership & Organizational Studies* 17, no. 1 (2010): 5–17.

Headey, Bruce and R. J. A. Muffels. "Towards a Theory of Medium-Term Life Satisfaction: Two-Way Causation Partly Explains Persistent Satisfaction or Dissatisfaction." *Social Indicators Research* 129, no. 2 (2016): 937–960.

Heckman, James J. and Tim D. Kautz. *Fostering and Measuring Skills: Interventions That Improve Character and Cognition*: National Bureau of Economic Research, 2013, doi:10.3386/w19656.

Heidemeier, Heike and Anja S. Göritz. "Individual Differences in How Work and Nonwork Life Domains Contribute to Life Satisfaction: Using Factor Mixture Modeling for Classification." *Journal of Happiness Studies* 14, no. 6 (2013): 1765–1788.

Hemingway, Ernest, *A Moveable Feast*. New York: Charles Scribner's Sons, 1964.

Henning, Peter J. "Treating Corporations as People." *New York Times*, May 26, 2015. https://www.nytimes.com/2015/05/27/business/dealbook/treating-corporations-as-people.html.

Heyes, Cecilia. "Where Do Mirror Neurons Come From?" *Neuroscience and Biobehavioral Reviews* 34, no. 4 (2010): 575–583.

Hong, Jihyung. "The Areas of Life Dissatisfaction and Their Relationships to Depression at Different Life Stages: Findings from a Nationally Representative Survey." *Psychology, Health & Medicine* 24, no. 3 (2019): 305–319.

Hooker, Christine I., Sara C. Verosky, Laura T. Germine, Robert T. Knight, and Mark D'Esposito. "Mentalizing about Emotion and Its Relationship to Empathy." *Social Cognitive and Affective Neuroscience* 3, no. 3 (2008): 204–217.

Huang, Jiatao, Hongbo Shi, and Wei Liu. "Emotional Intelligence and Subjective Well-being: Altruistic Behavior as a Mediator." *Social Behavior and Personality* 46, no. 5 (2018): 749–758.

Iacoboni, Marco. "Face to Face: The Neural Basis of Social Mirroring and Empathy." *Psychiatric Annals* 37, no. 4 (2007): 236–241.

Institute of Educational Sciences. https://ies.ed.gov/ncee/wwc/.

James, William. "The Energies of Men." *Science* 25, no. 635 (1907): 321–332.

Jin, Borae and Joohan Kim. "Grit, Basic Needs Satisfaction, and Subjective Well-being." *Journal of Individual Differences* 38, no. 1 (2017): 29–35.

Johnson, Spencer. *Who Moved My Cheese?* New York: G.P. Putnam's Sons, 1998.

Kaplan, Robert M., Jason M. Satterfield, and Raynard S. Kington. "Building a Better Physician: The Case for the New MCAT." *The New England Journal of Medicine* 366, no. 14 (2012): 1265–1268.

Karnitschnig, Matthew, Carrick Mollenkamp, and Dan Fitzpatrick, "Bank of America to Buy Merrill," *Wall Street Journal*, September 15, 2008, https://www.wsj.com/articles/SB122142278543033525.

Kelly, Dennis R., Michael D. Matthews, and Paul T. Bartone. "Grit and Hardiness as Predictors of Performance among West Point Cadets." *Military Psychology* 26, no. 4 (2017; 2014): 327–342.

Kelly, Kate and Serena Ng. "Bear Stearns Bails Out Fund with Big Loan." *Wall Street Journal*, June 23, 2007. https://www.wsj.com/articles/SB118252387194844899.

King Jr. Neil, and Sharon Terlep, "GM Collapses into Government's Arms," *Wall Street Journal*, June 2, 2009, https://www.wsj.com/articles/SB124385428627671889.

Lahti, Emilia. "Embodied Fortitude: An Introduction to the Finnish Construct of Sisu." *International Journal of Wellbeing* 9, no. 1 (2019): 61–82.

Lievens, Filip. "Adjusting Medical School Admission: Assessing Interpersonal Skills Using Situational Judgement Tests." *Medical Education* 47, no. 2 (2013): 182–189.

Libbrecht, Nele, Filip Lievens, Bernd Carette, and Stéphane Côté. "Emotional Intelligence Predicts Success in Medical School." *Emotion* 14, no. 1 (2014): 64–73.

Lykken, David and Auke Tellegen. "Happiness Is a Stochastic Phenomenon." *Psychological Science* 7, no. 3 (1996): 186–189.

Mackintosh, James. "Lehman's Lessons, 10 Years Later." *Wall Street Journal*, September 6, 2018. https://www.wsj.com/articles/lehmans-lessons-10-years-later-1536255748.

Maier, Steven F. and Martin E. P. Seligman. "Learned Helplessness at Fifty: Insights from Neuroscience." *Psychological Review* 123, no. 4 (2016): 349–367.

Marks, Stephen R. "Multiple Roles and Role Strain: Some Notes on Human Energy, Time and Commitment." *American Sociological Review* 42, no. 6 (1977): 921–936, doi:10.2307/2094577.

Marks, Stephen R. and Shelley M. MacDermid. "Multiple Roles and the Self: A Theory of Role Balance." *Journal of Marriage and Family* 58, no. 2 (1996): 417–432. doi:10.2307/353506.

Michael Beldoch, "Sensitivity to Expression of Emotional Meaning in Three Modes of Communication," *The Communication of Emotional*

Meaning, ed. J. R. Davitz and Michael Beldoch (Columbus, OH: McGraw-Hill; 1964), 31–42.

Karl Marx. *The Communist Manifesto*. New York: Penguin Classics, 2015.

Marušić, Berislav. *Evidence and Agency: Norms of Belief for Promising and Resolving*. Oxford: Oxford University Press, 2015.

Matthews, Gerald, Amanda K. Emo, Gregory Funke, Moshe Zeidner, Richard D. Roberts, Paul T. Costa, and Ralf Schulze. "Emotional Intelligence, Personality, and Task-Induced Stress." *Journal of Experimental Psychology: Applied* 12, no. 2 (2006): 96–107.

Mayer, John D., Richard D. Roberts, and Sigal G. Barsade. "Human Abilities: Emotional Intelligence." *Annual Review of Psychology* 59, no. 1 (2008): 507–536.

Michaels, Daniel. "Long-Dead Inventor Nikola Tesla Is Electrifying Hip Techies." *Wall Street Journal*, January 14, 2010, https://www.wsj.com/articles/SB10001424052748704362004575000841720318942.

Milston, Sashenka I., Eric J. Vanman, and Ross Cunnington. "Cognitive Empathy and Motor Activity during Observed Actions." *Neuropsychologia* 51, no. 6 (2013): 1103–1108.

Morton, Jennifer M. and Sarah K. Paul. "Grit." *Ethics* 129, no. 2 (2019): 175–203.

Myers, Chelsea A., Cheng Wang, Jessica M. Black, Nicolle Bugescu, and Fumiko Hoeft. "The Matter of Motivation: Striatal Resting-State Connectivity Is Dissociable between Grit and Growth Mindset." *Social Cognitive and Affective Neuroscience* 11, no. 10 (2016): 1521–1527.

Neumann, Jeannette. "Bear Stearns Fund Liquidators Sue Credit-Rating Firms." *Wall Street Journal,* July 10, 2013, https://www.wsj.com/articles/SB10001424127887323740804578597883074252160.l.

Nietzsche, Friedrich. *Basic Writings of Nietzsche.* New York: Modern Library, 2009.

———. *Twilight of the Idols,* 1889. Translated by Duncan Large. Oxford: Oxford Press, 1998.

Nietzsche, Friedrich. *Stanford Encyclopedia of Philosophy,* March 17, 2017, https://plato.stanford.edu/entries/nietzsche/.

Norton M. I. and D. Ariely, "Building a better America—One Wealth Quintile at a Time," *Perspectives on Psychological Science* 6 (2011): 9–12.

Oswald, Frederick L., Neal Schmitt, Brian H. Kim, Lauren J. Ramsay, and Michael A. Gillespie. "Developing a Biodata Measure and Situational Judgment Inventory as Predictors of College Student Performance." *Journal of Applied Psychology* 89, no. 2 (2004): 187–207.

Oxford English Dictionary Online. 3rd ed., 2021.

Palmer, Benjamin, Catherine Donaldson, and Con Stough. "Emotional Intelligence and Life Satisfaction." *Personality and Individual Differences* 33, no. 7 (2002): 1091–1100.

Pantzar, Katja. *The Finnish Way.* New York: TarcherParigree, 2018.

Pavot, William and Ed Diener. "The Satisfaction with Life Scale and the Emerging Construct of Life Satisfaction." *The Journal of Positive Psychology* 3, no. 2 (2008): 137–152.

Perkins-Gough, D. and Angela L. Duckworth. "The Significance of GRIT: A Conversation with Angela Lee Duckworth." *Educational Leadership* 71, no. 1 (2013): 14–20.

Peterson, Christopher, Nansook Park, and Martin E. P. Seligman. "Orientations to Happiness and Life Satisfaction: The Full Life versus the Empty Life." *Journal of Happiness Studies* 6, no. 1 (2005): 25–41.

Purushothaman, Rajagopalan. *Emotional Intelligence*. New Delhi: SAGE Publications, 2021.

Roberts, Brent W., Nathan R. Kuncel, Rebecca Shiner, Avshalom Caspi, and Lewis R. Goldberg. "The Power of Personality: The Comparative Validity of Personality Traits, Socioeconomic Status, and Cognitive Ability for Predicting Important Life Outcomes." *Perspectives on Psychological Science* 2, no. 4 (2007): 313–345.

Santrock, J. W. *Life-span Development*, 17th ed. New York: McGraw-Hill, 2015.

———. *Life-span Development*, 18th ed. McGraw-Hill: New York, 2021.

Sidel, Robin, Dennis K. Berman, and Kate Kelly, "J.P. Morgan Buys Bear in Fire Sale, as Fed Widens Credit to Avert Crisis." *Wall Street Journal*, March 17, 2008, https://www.wsj.com/articles/SB120569598608739825.

Sims, Tamara, Candice L. Hogan, and Laura L. Carstensen. "Selectivity as an Emotion Regulation Strategy: Lessons from Older Adults." *Current Opinion in Psychology* 3, (2015): 80–84.

Smith, Adam *The Wealth of Nations*. Oxford, England: Bibliomania.com Ltd, 2002, lccn.loc.gov/2002564559.

Solomon, Deborah, Damian Paletta, Jon Hilsenrath, and Aaron Lucchetti, "U.S. to Buy Stakes in Nation's Largest Banks," *Wall Street Journal*, October 14, 2008, https://www.wsj.com/articles/SB122390023840728367.

Stanley, Colleen. *Emotional Intelligence for Sales Leadership: The Secret to Building High-Performance Sales Teams*. New York: HarperCollins Leadership, 2020.

Stein, Steven and Howard E. Book. *The EQ Edge: Emotional Intelligence and Your Success*. Mississauga, Ontario: Jossey-Bass, 2011.

Steinberg, Julie. "J.P. Morgan to Pay $500 Million to Settle Lawsuit," *Wall Street Journal*, January 9, 2015, https://www.wsj.com/articles/j-p-morgan-to-pay-500-million-to-settle-lawsuit-1420836735.

Stoffel, Jaclyn M. and Jeff Cain. "Review of Grit and Resilience Literature within Health Professions Education." *American Journal of Pharmaceutical Education* 82, no. 2 (2018): 6150–134.

Swami, Viren, Tomas Chamorro-Premuzic, Dhachayani Sinniah, Thambu Maniam, Kumaraswami Kannan, Debbi Stanistreet, and Adrian Furnham. "General Health Mediates the Relationship between Loneliness, Life Satisfaction and Depression: A Study with Malaysian Medical Students." *Social Psychiatry and Psychiatric Epidemiology* 42, no. 2 (2007): 161–166.

"Teachers Defend 'No-Zero' Grading Policy." *WPTV News*, September 26, 2018. <https://www.youtube.com/watch?v=I4mXsbpE5nA>.

Tiffin, Paul A. and Lewis W. Paton. "When I Say … Emotional Intelligence." *Medical Education* 54, no. 7 (2020): 598–599.

Tominey, Shauna L., Elisabeth C. O'Bryon, Susan E. Rivers, and Sharon Shapses. "Teaching Emotional Intelligence in Early Childhood." *YC Young Children* 72, no. 1 (2017): 6–14.

Vanhove, Adam J., Mitchel N. Herian, Alycia L. U. Perez, Peter D. Harms, and Paul B. Lester. "Can Resilience Be Developed at Work? A Meta-Analytic Review of Resilience-Building Programme Effectiveness." *Journal of Occupational and Organizational Psychology* 89, no. 2 (2016): 278–307.

Vela, Javier C., James Ikonomopoulos, Karina Hinojosa, Stacey L. Gonzalez, Omar Duque, and Megan Calvillo. "The Impact of Individual, Interpersonal, and Institutional Factors on Latina/o College Students' Life Satisfaction." *Journal of Hispanic Higher Education* 15, no. 3 (2016): 260–276.

Vela, Javier C., Ming-Tsan P. Lu, A. Stephen Lenz, Miranda C. Savage, and Rebekah Guardiola. "Positive Psychology and Mexican American College Students' Subjective Well-being and Depression." *Hispanic Journal of Behavioral Sciences* 38, no. 3 (2016): 324–340.

Vogt, Stefan, Giovanni Buccino, Afra M. Wohlschläger, Nicola Canessa, N. Jon Shah, Karl Zilles, Simon B. Eickhoff, Hans-Joachim Freund, Giacomo Rizzolatti, and Gereon R. Fink. "Prefrontal Involvement in Imitation Learning of Hand Actions: Effects of Practice and Expertise." *NeuroImage* 37, no. 4 (2007): 1371–1383.

Von Culin, Katherine R., Eli Tsukayama, and Angela L. Duckworth. "Unpacking Grit: Motivational Correlates of Perseverance and Passion for Long-Term Goals." *The Journal of Positive Psychology* 9, no. 4 (2014): 306–312.

Wang, Song, Ming Zhou, Taolin Chen, Xun Yang, Guangxiang Chen, Meiyun Wang, and Qiyong Gong. "Grit and the Brain: Spontaneous Activity of the Dorsomedial Prefrontal Cortex Mediates the Relationship between the Trait Grit and Academic

Performance." *Social Cognitive and Affective Neuroscience* 12, no. 3 (2017): 452–460.

Wodwaski, Nadine and Courtney, Renee. "Emotional Intelligence: An Unspoken Competency in Home Care," *Home Healthcare Now* 38, no. 5 (2020): 286.

Wynne, Sharon A. *Highly Qualified Teachers: Florida Educational Leadership Examination.* Melrose: XAMonline, Inc., 2018.

Wolters, Christopher A. and Maryam Hussain. "Investigating Grit and Its Relations with College Students' Self-Regulated Learning and Academic Achievement." *Metacognition and Learning* 10, no. 3 (2015): 293–311.

Zeidner, M., RD Roberts, and G. Matthews. "The Science of Emotional Intelligence: Current Consensus and Controversies." *European Psychologist* 13, no. 1 (2008): 64–78.

Zibel, Alan, and Jeffrey Sparshott, "TARP Watchdog: Big Banks Got Unfair Advantage." *Wall Street Journal,* March 17, 2011. https://www.wsj.com/articles/SB10001424052748703818204576206482220073322.

CPSIA information can be obtained
at www.ICGtesting.com
Printed in the USA
BVHW071635060422
633551BV00006B/207